All
Will Be
Well

All Will Be Well

A Gathering of Healing Prayers

Edited by
Lyn Klug

Augsburg
MINNEAPOLIS

ALL WILL BE WELL
A Gathering of Healing Prayers

Copyright © 1998 Augsburg Fortress. All rights reserved. Except for brief quotations in critical articles or reviews, no part of this book may be reproduced in any manner without prior written permission from the publisher. Write to: Permissions, Augsburg Fortress, Box 1209, Minneapolis, MN 55440.

Cover design by Elizabeth Boyce. Interior design by Michelle L. Norstad.
Cover and interior art by Carolyn Brunelle; *Faunal Vessel IV*, acrylic on paper, 32" x 45", used by permission.

ISBN 0-8066-3729-3

Please see page 164 for copyright acknowledgments.

The paper used in this publication meets the minimum requirements of American National Standard for Information Sciences—Permanence of Paper for Printed Library Materials, ANSI Z329.48-1984.

Manufactured in the U.S.A.   AF 9-3729

02   01   00   99   98   1   2   3   4   5   6   7   8   9   10

Contents

∾

Introduction

When we or our loved ones experience illness—in body, mind, or spirit—our resources are stretched to the utmost. We struggle with feelings of fear, anxiety, helplessness, and desperation. We do what we can, but often it just is not enough. We need help from beyond ourselves.

Since biblical times, believers have looked to God for healing and wholeness. Today, there is a new openness to spiritual healing expressed by doctors, psychologists, and those who suffer. While we are grateful for all the life-giving scientific advances in medicine, we know there are ways of healing that are beyond the reach of science. Healing remains a mystery involving our minds, souls, relationships, personal histories, the communities in which we live, and the earth itself.

At times prayer comes to us spontaneously. We find it easy to turn in faith to a loving God, expressing in our own words what is on our hearts and minds. But at other times we are overcome by fatigue, stress, doubts, and confusion. The words will not come. At times like this we can turn to those who have gone before us on the road of suffering. Those who have written about their healings have left us words that can speak for us, helping us express what is otherwise inexpressible, renewing our trust in God the Healer, and showing us that we are not alone, no matter what we may be feeling.

Trust is not easy. The prayers of many great believers include cries of pain, despair, and doubt. But those who have been honest to God in their worst moments allow us to be honest in ours, opening the way for healing. Some wise prayers enable us to see things from a new perspective, others to give thanks for the good that is present even in the midst of pain. Most important, other people's prayers move us into our own. We speak our true thoughts and feelings. We listen; some prayers become a word from God to us. Best of all may be the times when these words lead us to rest silently in the presence of God.

Prayer, whether written or flowing freely from the heart, releases the healing power of God into our situation. The results of our prayer may not always correspond to our wishes, but we trust that God's gift to us is always love, God's desire is always what is best for us and our loved ones, God's vision is always wider and wiser than our own. We anchor our faith on the hope that in God's good time and in God's way, "All will be well."

How to Use This Book
Books of written prayers can be used in many ways, whether you are praying for yourself or for a friend or family member. The Spirit of God will lead you to use this book in ways that are most beneficial for you. Here are some ways to begin:

• Read the book through or browse the sections that attract you, stopping to reflect on those prayers that connect with your experience.

• Use the prayers you need at this time, and let the others be. At some time in the future, those prayers may become yours as well.

• Adapt the prayers to your own life situation or that of your loved ones.

• Respond to the prayers in a journal, beginning an ongoing dialogue with God that can renew your spirit and help you make good choices in difficult times.

• Share the prayers with those you love and those for whom you pray. Include prayers in letters you write or leave them at the bedside of those you visit.

• Use the book as a resource for a prayer circle, healing ministry, or spirituality group.

Because each of us is a unique person at a particular place in our spiritual journey, we must find our own ways to pray, but we trust that the Spirit of God leads us in that search. When we are in great need, we seek until we find what truly helps us, and God sends blessings we never could have found on our own. Books like this can be our companions in the search for healing.

May God be with us as we seek healing for ourselves, our loved ones, and the world. May God bless us with the hope that in spite of illness, distress, and tears, all, indeed, will be well.

Let Comfort Come

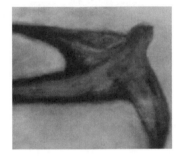

Prayers for
Physical Healing

$\mathcal{A}$lmighty God, you are the source of health and healing, the spirit of calm, and the central peace of the universe. We ask that you would fill us with such an awareness of your presence within that we may have complete confidence in you. In all pain and weariness and anxiety may we rest in your protecting care; may we know ourselves to be encircled by your loving power so that we may allow you to give us health and strength and peace, through Jesus Christ, our Lord. Amen

—*Avery Brooke*

$\mathcal{M}$erciful God,
Loving Mother,
Guiding Light.
Let comfort come this night
    for every wound and distress
    for every sorrow and uncertainty:
Your love shines upon us;
Your love will guard our rest.

—*Daniel J. McGill*

*J*ust for today,
What does it matter, O Lord, if the future is dark?
To pray now for tomorrow—I am not able.
Keep my heart only for today,
  give me your protection today,
  grant me your light—
  just for today.
  —*Saint Therese of Lisieux, France (1873–1897)*

*F*rom moment to moment one can bear much.
  —*Teresa of Avila, Spain (1515–1582)*

*M*y God—equally present
In darkness as in light,
Stand by me!
Allow me, yes, to suffer and be hurt,
But not to be broken or destroyed.
Allow me to be bruised,
But not my spirit to be overcome.
I know of suffering and I do not fear it.
I only fear my strength to carry it.
I ask not to escape from the threats and the pain,
I ask that I might carry them
With grace,
With hope,
With love.
—*Edwina Gateley*

*H*elp me to be brave.
Help me to be hopeful.
Help me to face cheerfully and openly—rather than
reluctantly and resentfully—whatever is coming next,
wherever it is that I am going.
—*Joan Bel Geddes*

$\mathcal{P}$raying a Bible Text

Repeated slowly many times, then silently many times, allowing the meaning to deepen into feeling, holding the attention on the text whenever it strays away, until at last the mind is silent and I experience the truth of the promise of which the text speaks.

Peace I leave with you, my peace I give unto you.

It is I, be not afraid.

Abide in me and let me abide in you.

Underneath are the everlasting arms.

I am with you always.

In quietness and confidence shall be your strength.

I have made, and I will bear.

Your ears shall hear a word behind you, saying,
this is the way, walk in it.

I will never leave you nor forsake you.
    —George Appleton, England (1902–1993)

$\mathcal{J}$esus,
you wasted no time agonizing over
the great wound of pain and suffering in creation,
or in asking who dealt this wound.
You simply accepted it as the mystery of existence
and then devoted your life to healing it.
The crowd read in your eyes God's love
for them in their miserable condition
and flocked to you. The crowd laid bare
its painful, suffering wound,
and you touched the wound with your hand,
your most personal human hand—
and healed it.

No gospel of suffering in the Gospels, then—
just you—God's Yes to a suffering world.
No illumination of pain and suffering in the Gospels—
just you, God's I Am Love,
radiantly and utterly illuminated.
    —*Edna Hong*

Some people find the imagination a useful tool in prayer. Picture Jesus healing people, and then see him walking toward you, looking at you with deep compassion, and stretching out his hands toward you. You could imagine that Jesus takes both your hands in his. Feel the warmth; the love; the sense of security, come what may. There is a Celtic encircling prayer which you could say as you imagine this:

I place my hands in yours, Lord,
I place my hands in yours.
I place my will in yours, Lord,
I place my will in yours.
I place my days in yours, Lord,
I place my days in yours.
I place my thoughts in yours, Lord,
I place my thoughts in yours.
I place my heart in yours, Lord,
I place my heart in yours.
I place my hands in yours, Lord,
I place my hands in yours.
—*Angela Ashwin*

I experienced it again today.
You were suddenly there
with your surprising presence.

You were suddenly there
without any visible reason,
without my having done anything,
without preparation,
without warning.
Suddenly you were there
with your complete joy,
with the relaxation which emanates from you,
with the sense you put back into life.

There you are
and I can only smile
at how connected everything is in my life.
        —*Ulrich Schaffer*

*W*e cannot fall beneath the arms of God.
However low we fall,
they are still underneath us.
        —*William Penn (1644–1718)*

*D*ear God,
The pain of this life is more than I can bear.
I feel as though death would be better.
My thoughts are dark, my sorrows huge.
I feel as though I shall not endure, and there is
    no one and nothing to turn to now.
My hurt is so big.
I cannot handle this.
If You can, dear God, please do.
If You can, please do.
Amen.

—*Marianne Williamson*

*J*esus Christ, if you had not cried
"My God, my God,
Why hast Thou forsaken me?"
I would be an atheist.

—*Thomas R. Heath, O.P.*

*H*elp of the tired ones,
I am in need tonight—
so weary I can hardly think
or pray aright;
but you have known the toil,
the grief, the strain
of human suffering,
and felt the pain
of utter weariness—
the sting of tears, fatigue—
and so you know my need.

I have no words to say,
but in my heart
I pray.
　　　　—Mary Esther Burgoyne

*M*ay the God who listens to our hearts and enters into our pain
bless us and all who are in need with the comfort and quiet of Her
gentle presence, now and always. Amen.
　　　　—Marchiene Vroon Rienstra

$\mathcal{D}$ear Lord, in the midst of much inner turmoil and restlessness, there is a consoling thought: maybe you are working in me in a way I cannot yet feel, experience or understand. My mind is not able to concentrate on you, my heart is not able to remain centered, and it seems as if you are absent and have left me alone. But in faith I cling to you. I believe that your Spirit reaches deeper and further than my mind or heart, and that profound movements are not the first to be noticed.

Therefore, Lord, I promise I will not run away, not give up, not stop praying, even when it all seems useless, pointless, and a waste of time and effort. I want to let you know that I love you even though I do not feel loved by you, and that I hope in you even though I often experience despair. Let this be a little dying I can do with you and for you as a way of experiencing some solidarity with the millions in this world who suffer far more than I do. Amen.

—*Henri Nouwen (1932–1996)*

Almighty God, whose most dear Son went not up to joy but first he suffered pain, and entered not into glory before he was crucified: mercifully grant that we, walking in the way of the cross, may find it none other than the way of life and peace; through Jesus Christ your Son our Lord, who lives and reigns with you and the Holy Spirit, one God, for ever and ever. Amen.

   —Book of Common Prayer

Lord, let me make sickness itself a prayer.

   —Saint Francis de Sales, France (1567–1622)

O Lord, it has been a while since I've walked on grass or seen the stars in the sky. So many silent and restless nights, so many long and boring days in a hospital bed. At first I was too sick to care, but now I am getting impatient to go home. I get upset about my dependency, my setbacks, my slow progress. At times even the people who are trying to do their best to help me irritate me and get on my nerves. It's not really their fault. It's just me, that I can only take so much and then I have to let it out. But since, O Lord, you have taken me this far, since you have given me enough patience to endure, I pray again that you heal that which still needs to be healed in me. May I soon breathe fresh air and enjoy the atmosphere of my own home. I ask this in Jesus' name. Amen.

—*Father Arnaldo Pangrazzi*

T hank you, O God, for all the people who have looked after me today . . .
Into your strong hands I place all the patients in this ward . . .
the night staff on duty tonight . . .
my loved ones whose names I now mention . . .
myself, with my fears, my worries and my hopes . . .
Help me to sleep, thinking of you and your promises. Amen.

—*Christian Publicity Organization, England*

Bless her for not saying, "you look terrific";
   (I would have to fib back, "I feel pretty good, too.")
Bless her for not talking about her aches and pains;
   (I sense they are probably more painful than mine.)
Bless her for her smile that lights up my room;
   (One of those genuine smiles that are so rare today.)
But most of all, God, bless this dear thoughtful soul
      for sneaking me a corned beef on rye.
      —*John V. Chervokas*

They don't call.
They don't come.
I feel invisible, forgotten.
I know they are busy.
I've been busy myself.
But . . . it means so much.
Maybe they don't realize it,
as I didn't, back when . . .
But, right now,
I feel forgotten
by those I love most.
Empty, when I'd rather be full,
is how I come to You this day, my God.
      —*Marlene Halpin, Dominican*

Breathing deeply and slowly, silently say part of a line as you inhale, and part as you exhale. As the prayer is repeated, painful areas in the body relax and God's peace is received into the deep levels of the mind.

The Lord is my shepherd. I shall not want.

O Lord make haste to help me.

Jesus, Healer, make me whole.

I'm afraid, Lord. I need you.

Please give me the strength I need.

Whatever will heal me, please send it now.

Holy Spirit, breathe in me.

Christ be with me, Christ within me,
Christ behind me, Christ before me,
Christ beside me, Christ to win me,
Christ to comfort and restore me.

*J*esus breathed on them, and said to them, "Receive the Holy Spirit."
—*John 20:22*

*L*et everything that breathes praise the Lord!
—*Psalm 150:6*

*G*ently and lightly massage the hands, face, and neck. Claim with trust the presence of Jesus Christ, the incarnate love of God, always with you. Relax your body, close your eyes, and picture around you some light, color, water, warmth, breeze, or other symbol of God's energizing and enfolding presence.

Listen to any signals from the body of physical discomfort, pain, tension, unease. Focus on that part of your body, feeling it breathing in and out as if that part had its own separate breathing apparatus. Let that body part breathe slowly for several minutes. Visualize God's surrounding light or breath flowing in and out of that area.

When it feels right, move on to another area, letting that area breathe in and out. This is a powerful pain reliever. Now let your whole body breathe slowly, gently from the soles of the feet to the top of the head. Don't gasp or push it.

Now just sit quietly, leaning on the strength of God, letting God's life-giving breath flow in and out of your body. Give thanks, and when ready, open your eyes.

—*Flora Slosson Wuellner*

All is ill and very ill
but all will be well again.
Time will heal,
time will mend.
All will be well again!
 —*Edna Hong*

And so our Good Lord answered to all the questions and doubts which I could raise, saying most comfortingly: I may make all things well, and I can make all things well, and I shall make all things well, . . . And you will see yourself that every kind of thing will be well . . . And in these . . . words, God wishes us to be enclosed in rest and in peace.
 —*Julian of Norwich, England (1342–1419)*

"That which is impossible for you is not impossible to me:
I will preserve my word in all things and I will make all things well."

This is the Great Deed that Our God will do.

Our faith is grounded in God's Word and we must let this trust be.
How it will be done we will not know until it is done,
because God wants us to be at ease and at peace,
not troubled or kept from enjoying God.

God does not want us to be burdened because of sorrows
and tempests that happen in our lives,
because it has always been so before miracles happen.
    —*Julian of Norwich, England (1342–1419)*

Once life has almost been taken from you,
When for some strange reason
you emerge from death
and blink with new eyes
upon the old, almost forgotten universe,
then you can understand once more
the value of sea and stars,
of happiness uncontainable,
the sheer relief and delight of being alive
that turns your eyes repeatedly upwards
with thanksgiving,
then straight outward
declaring peace over and over again
to those who with heads bent low
see mud, not stars.

 —*Kathy Keay, England (1954–1994)*

*M*ay the Light shine on all your days.
It is there, despite illness, defeat, and tears.
It is eternal.

 —*Harvey Stower*

The Burdens We Carry

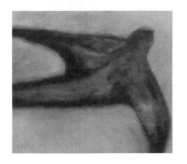

Prayers for
Mental and
Emotional Healing

$\mathcal{G}$od of our life,
there are days when the burdens we carry
chafe our shoulders and weigh us down;
when the road seems dreary and endless,
the skies gray and threatening;
when our lives have no music in them,
and our hearts are lonely,
and our souls have lost their courage.

Flood the path with light, we beseech Thee;
turn our eyes to where the skies are full of promise;
tune our hearts to brave music;
give us the sense of comradeship with heroes and saints of every age;
and so quicken our spirits that we may be able to encourage
the souls of all who journey with us on the road to life,
to Thy honor and glory.

    —Saint Augustine, North Africa (354–430)

I am, O God, a jumbled mass of motives; One moment I am ador-ing you, and the next I am shaking my fist at you. I vacillate between mounting hope, and deepening despair. I am full of faith, and full of doubt. I want the best for others, and am jealous when they get it. Even so, God, I will not run from your presence. Nor will I pretend to be what I am not. Thank you for accepting me with all my contra-dictions. Amen.

    —*Richard J. Foster*

O God, Giver of Life, Bearer of Pain, Maker of Love,
you are able to accept in us what we
cannot even acknowledge;
you are able to name in us what we cannot bear to speak of;
you are able to hold in your memory
what we have tried to forget;
you are able to hold out to us
the glory that we cannot conceive of.
Reconcile us through your cross
to all that we have rejected in our selves,
that we may find no part of your creation
to be alien or strange to us,
and that we ourselves may be made whole.
Through Jesus Christ, our lover and our friend. Amen.

    —*Janet Morley, England*

1 keep projecting my present condition onto the future. If I feel dark, the future looks dark; if I feel bright, the future looks bright. But who am I to know what life will be like for me tomorrow, next week, next year, or ten years from now? Even more, who am I to know who you will be for me in the year ahead? O Lord, I will not bind you with my own limited and limiting ideas and feelings. You can do so many things with me, things that might seem totally impossible to me. I want at least to remain open to the free movement of your Spirit in my life. Why do I keep saying to myself: "I will never be a saint. I will never be able to overcome my impulses and desires." If I keep saying that, I might prevent you from healing and touching me deeply. O Lord, let me remain free to let you come whenever and however you desire. Amen.

—*Henri Nouwen (1932–1996)*

O Love unspeakable and full of glory, whose majesty is not to destroy, but to save, save us from ourselves. Our past relentlessly pursues us. Days that we thought dead live over again; deeds that we deemed buried meet us on the way; be thou our defense, O our God.

Fill up that which our lives have left behind. Undo that which we have done amiss. Repair the places we have wasted, bind the hearts we have wounded. Dry the eyes which we have flooded. Make the evil we have done work for good, so that we ourselves would not know it.

Take up our yesterdays into thine own golden light and transfigure them there, that we may learn with joyful surprise how ever against our wills we were laboring together with thee; so shall our former selves find us no more. Amen.

—*Author unknown*

*G*ive me a candle of the Spirit, O God, as I go down into the deeps of my being. Show me the hidden things, the creatures of my dreams, the storehouse of forgotten memories and hurts. Take me down to the spring of my life and tell me my nature and my name. Give me freedom to grow, so that I may become that self, the seed of which you planted in me at my making. Out of the deeps I cry to you, O God.

—*George Appleton, England (1902–1993)*

1 carry the sorrows
of my years
within me.
Often,
not even loved ones
know.

Some burdens
have gotten lighter
with time.

Others
weigh heavier still.

I give my secret pain
to you, God.
Help me!
　　　—*Pat Corrick Hinton*

*N*ow you too may kneel before the Christ child to leave at his feet
those unseen, secret things that may be left nowhere else but there.
And having visited the holy place, you too, like those three visitors
of old, may go on your way made new.
　　　—*Paul Flucke, Canada*

This life is not a state of being righteous,
but rather, of growth in righteousness;
not a state of being healthy, but a period of healing;
not a state of being, but becoming;
not a state of rest, but of exercise and activity.
We are not yet what we shall be, but we grow towards it;
the process is not yet finished, but is still going on;
this life is not the end, it is the way to a better.
All does not yet shine with glory;
nevertheless, all is being purified. (2 Corinthians 3:18)
    —Martin Luther, Germany (1483–1546)

Holy Spirit,
giving life to all life,
moving all creatures,
root of all things,
washing them clean,
wiping out their mistakes,
healing their wounds,
you are our true life,
luminous, wonderful,
awakening the heart
from its ancient sleep.
    —Hildegard of Bingen, Germany (1098–1179);
      translated by Stephen Mitchell

When I was small the words would not come.
I could not speak.
The people looked at me and asked about me
and wondered about me,
but I couldn't speak.
I was silent, and they shook their heads and walked away.
Now I am grown, and words come.
I speak.
The people look at me and ask about me
and wonder about me still, and I speak.
I say, "Yes, children do get hurt." I say, "No, I don't understand."
I say, "child sexual abuse." I say, "incest." I say, "pain."
Then they look beyond me and long to be gone,
away from my painful truths.
They shake their heads and walk away.
But you, Jesus, you tell stories of people who listened.
You tell stories of those who stopped and stooped
to hear the pain.
Samaritans, approaching the wounded.
Willing to feel pain as they listen to pain.
You tell stories of seeing, of hearing, of neighbors, of love.
And you, Jesus. You say, "Tell me."
You say, "Speak. I am not afraid to feel."
You approach the pain.
You teach me that pain will not destroy.
When the storm is over, the resurrection begins.
—*Catherine J. Foote*

*D*ear God,
I feel such pain, anxiety, and depression.
I know this is not Your will for me,
and yet my mind is held in chains by fear and paranoia.
I surrender my life, right now, to You.
Take the entire mess, all of it,
now too complicated to explain to anyone
but known by You in each detail.
Do what I cannot do.
Lift me up.
Give me a new chance.
Show me a new light.
Make me a new person.
Dear God,
This depression frightens me.
Dear God,
Please bring me peace.
Amen.
     —Marianne Williamson

I was terrified I'd break down.
I did.
It didn't matter.
     —Rosalind M. Baker, England

*D*ear Higher Power,
Show me the Miracle of your Love in this situation,
because I only see resentment and hatred.
Show me the Miracle of your Healing,
because I cannot stop seeing what is diseased.
Give me the Miracle of your Release,
because I am afraid to let go.
Bring me the Miracle of your Faith,
because I am overwhelmed by doubt and confusion.
Show me the Light of your Care,
because I feel alone and lost in darkness.
Show me the Miracle of your Vision,
for I see myself and others with eyes
of judgment and quiet condemnation.
Show me the Miracle of Life,
because I have been fighting and do not trust it.
Be the Miracle in my life. Amen.
  —*Geraldine Mosley*

*L*ord,
first let us hear the voice
crying in the wilderness of our own hearts.
  —*Based on some words of George Fox, England (1624–1691)*

God, I just want to talk to you, I just want to open my soul to you. I don't want to try to say it right. I don't want to meet someone else's expectations of what I should say or what I should believe. I just want to talk to you.

I sit sometimes in a deep well. I can't get out. I'm so tired of the struggle. I ache. I want to stop time and spend time with me. But time moves on and takes me with it.

God, I'm too tired to hold on, and I don't know any way out. This aching human part of me, what do I do with this? God, you have abandoned me. I cannot pretend that I feel you here. I cannot pretend that I'm OK. All I can do is hold on and hope this feeling will pass. All I can do is trust that it will stop and when I pass through, you will be there on the other side. Amen.

—*Catherine J. Foote*

Go, and know that the Lord goes with you: let him lead you each day into the quiet place of your heart, where he will speak with you; know that he loves you and watches over you—that he listens to you in gentle understanding, that he is with you always, wherever you are and however you may feel: and the blessings of God—Father, Son and Holy Spirit—be yours for ever.

—*Author unknown*

W ho can boast of being free?
Who has not got secret prisons,
invisible chains, all the more constricting
the less they are apparent?
  —*Dom Helder Camara, Brazil*

L ord,
free us from falling into the sin
of believing that the slavery in Egypt
is better than the struggles in the desert.
  —*Tómas H. Téllez, Nicaragua*

W ell, my poor heart, here we are,
fallen into the ditch which we
had made so firm a resolution to avoid;
Oh!! let us rise and leave it forever.
Courage! Henceforth, let us be more on our guard.
God will help us, we shall do well enough!
  —*Saint Francis de Sales, France (1567–1622)*

Take my weakness, God.
Take my failures, my sins, my dishonesties,
lies, pride, and lusts.
God knows—you know—
I can't do anything with them.
So, for Christ's sake, take them.
And give me, I pray you,
not so much a clean spirit,
nor a pure heart,
nor a sense of forgiveness—
give me a sense of you,
of you in me, and I in you.
Then shall I be strong to be for you.
Simply to be.
    —*John B. Coburn*

God, whose name is Truth—
I thirst for honesty, integrity, sincerity.
There are lies here.
There are opaque places in my spirit.
There are delusions, chains, deceptions, clouds.
Give me the grace to let these shadows go,
to find your Truth already hidden in my heart.
    —*Holly Jo Turnquist Fischer*

Dear God, I feel that I have wasted my life, thrown away my resources, taken too much time to gather my strengths. Now, dear God, I feel it is too late for me. My age, my weaknesses, the lies and betrayals of time gone by, all make me seem a lesser talent. And only You, dear God, know the love in my heart and how much I want to serve, how much I have to give. I need a miracle, a new beginning, which only You can give me. Please, dear God, I give my life to You. Please bring together my talents. Please increase my gifts and use them for Your purposes. I surrender my future. Make it unlike my past. Thank You very much. Amen.

—*Marianne Williamson*

My mind is happy today in the thought that I am God's child in God's world to do God's work within God's will.

This is to be a day of joy and optimism and courage. From all negative thoughts my mind resolutely turns away.

The Spirit of God is working in my body to bring health, and in my mind to bring serenity, and I am one with that Spirit. I am not apart from, or disapproved of, or turned away by, God. No impostor-fears shall let me think I am.

I affirm the reality of health and peace and love within me because God dwells therein.

—*Leslie Weatherhead, England (1883–1975)*

Dear God: Help me to admit mistakes freely without feeling shame, and to recognize that they come to teach me. Help me to find my own voice, to say what I mean and mean what I say. Help me to see the good and to laugh at myself and at life more. Help me to discover my gifts and honor the uniqueness of others. Help me to accept who I am, a beloved and special being in Your eyes. And above all, help me to remain patient and gentle with myself.

—*Robert and Janet Ellsworth*

As swimmers dare
to lie face to the sky
and water bears them,
as hawks rest upon air
and air sustains them,
so would I learn to attain
freefall, and float
into Creator Spirit's deep embrace,
knowing no effort earns
that all-surrounding grace.
   —*Denise Levertov (1923–1997)*

*S*ometimes
I go about pitying myself
while I am carried by
The wind
Across the sky.
   —*Chippewa Song*

O Lord, please send me someone who can take the time to notice me, someone who can visit me to break the silence of my day, someone who can put her hands into my heart and draw out into the light my inner longings, someone who can listen with their eyes and hear my hunger, someone who can smile at me, someone who can reflect with me. Someone, I am lonely for you today. Why do you run away from me? Is time too short for you to love? What do you see in me that scares you?

Remember, Someone, that if you take time to hear my silence, I will take time to unfold my presence; if you take time to touch my pain, I will take time to give you purpose; if you take time to accept my seasons, I will take time to change your heart.

Someone, don't be afraid about what to say, just stay with me and hold my hand. Tomorrow I might not pass this way again. Amen.

—*Father Arnaldo Pangrazzi*

Dear Lord Jesus,
I don't know who I am,
I don't know where I am,
and I don't know what I am,
but please love me.

—*Prayer of a sufferer from Alzheimer's disease*

*B*reath prayers for inner healing can be prayed anywhere, anytime, especially when we are distressed or discouraged. Slow, deep breathing calms the mind and body, and the prayer turns us toward God.

> Out of the depths have I cried unto Thee O Lord.
> Lord hear my voice.

> Where the Spirit of the Lord is, there is freedom.

> Lord of life, send my roots rain.

> I love you, O Lord, my strength.

> Show me, O Lord, the path of life.

*Y*ou can also pray while you work. Work doesn't stop prayer, and prayer doesn't stop work. It requires only that small raising of the mind to God. "I love you, God, I trust you, I believe in you, I need you now," small things like that. They are wonderful prayers.

—*Mother Teresa, India (1910–1997)*

*W*hen I come to the end of my prayers, I find that there are
   prayers I still need.
A prayer for the courage to speak the truth.
Another prayer for the pain.
A prayer for the sadness.
A prayer for fears.
A prayer for the anger that sometimes smolders
   and sometimes burns.
A prayer for justice and for grace.
A prayer for strength to keep telling my story,
to keep moving toward wholeness, to keep moving toward you.
A prayer for wisdom.
Another prayer for love. Amen.
   —*Catherine J. Foote*

Thy Kingdom Come

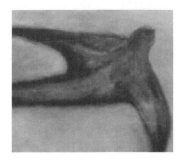

Prayers for
the Healing
of Community

*T*hy kingdom come, thy will be done, on earth, as it is in heaven.
—*Matthew 6:10*

O Lord, whose power to heal was tested against the power which destroys, and proved stronger: open our eyes to the signs of your strength in this modern world, and open our hearts to the Kingdom of God, which has come upon us; through the power of your Spirit. Amen.
—*Susan Williams*

Bless your people, Lord,
who have walked too long in this night of pain.
For the child has no more tears to cry
and the old people no song of joy to sing,
and the blood of our youth drains away in the gutters.
The cry from the cross is heard throughout the land.
The pain in your nailed hands is carried by the worker.
Terrible thirst is in the mouth of the farmer,
too many women mourn the loss of their sons,
and all the earth is turned into another Calvary.
With your spirit, Lord we cry for peace.
With your spirit, we struggle to be free.
        —*National Council of Churches of the Philippines*

Lord Jesus, you were awakened by the cry of your disciples on a storm-tossed sea. Hear also our cry for help. There is no justice in our land for the weak and powerless, because the powerful and the strong have decided what is and what is not right and just. We, the minority of the humble and meek are tired of crying for justice and peace. How much longer must the mighty dominate and the weak suffer? Bring your justice, and grant us your peace. Let your kingdom become a reality on this earth.
        —*Sri Lanka*

*L*ord Jesus Christ, help us not to fall in love with the night that covers us but through the darkness to watch for you as well as to work for you; to dream and hunger in the dark for the light of you. Help us to know that the madness of God is saner than men and that nothing that God has wrought in this world was ever possible.

Give us back the great hope again that the future is yours, that not even the world can hide you from us forever, that at the end the One who came will come back in power to work joy in us stronger even than death. Amen.

—Frederick Buechner

*F*rom the mingled light and shadow of hope
I greet you, Lord, God.

—Dom Helder Camara, Brazil

All the broken hearts shall rejoice;
all those who are heavy laden,
whose eyes are tired and do not see,
shall be lifted up
to meet with the motherly healer.
The battered souls and bodies shall be healed;
the hungry shall be fed;
the imprisoned shall be free;
all her earthly children shall regain joy
in the reign of the just and loving one
coming for you
coming for me
in this time
in this world.
  —*Sun Ai Park, Korea*

May those who sow in tears
  reap with shouts of joy.
  —*Psalm 126*

1 believe that God
has the whole world
in his hands.

He is not a bystander
at the pain of the world.
He does not stand
like Peter,
wringing his hands
in the shadows,
but is there,
in the dock,
on the rack,
high on the gallows tree.

He is in the pain
of the lunatic,
the tortured,
those wracked by grief.
His is the blood
that flows in the gutter.
His are the veins burned by heroin,
his the lungs choked by AIDS.

His is the heart
broken by suffering,
his the despair
of the mute,
the oppressed,
the man with the gun to his head.
He is the God of Paradox.
　　—*Sheila Cassidy, England*

*G*od of all good life, on our journey toward Easter, cleanse our hearts of every desire to mimic the violence of wrongs that befall us. Save us from becoming the evil we hate. Save us from denial of abuses which daily crucify Christ afresh. Drive away the chilling cold, the wintry frost, of numbing detachment from others' pain, and our own hurts, also. Breathe, O breathe Your empowering Spirit into the troubled hearts of Your children who wish they could wish to love but cannot.

　　Hear our prayer, in the name of Jesus, the Shining Way, the Truth, and the Life. Amen.
　　—*Obie Wright Jr.*

Oh Lord, once I was smart enough to know a just war when I saw it, the kind of war you would approve of. I am not so smart anymore. Every war looks evil to me now. And even the war well begun becomes evil before it's over. So let us have no more of just wars; they are the worst kind. Now, at last, give us a just peace. It's time, Lord.

Past time. Time for Shalom. Shalom for our breaking hearts. It's time.
—*Lewis B. Smedes*

Lead me from death to life, from falsehood to truth.
Lead me from despair to hope, from fear to trust.
Lead me from hate to love, from war to peace.
Let peace fill our heart, our world, our universe.
Peace. Peace. Peace.
—*Satish Kumar*

Goodness is stronger than evil;
Love is stronger than hate;
Light is stronger than darkness;
Life is stronger than death;
Victory is ours through Him who loves us.
—*Desmond Tutu, South Africa*

*B*less, O God, my enemies with sunshine.
Upon their crops come shining.
May green grass grow in their meadows,
Sweet crops within their fields;
Send rain upon their soil,
Fill their children with joy,
Bless their grandparents with peace.
May every woman of them know delight;
May every man of them be loved.
May the birds of their air never hear bombs;
May their rivers run clean,
       their air smell sweet in the morning.

May all things with life be blessed!
For if my enemy is not blessed,
How can I, O Lord, be blessed?
How can I?
For earth shall cry if they shall weep,
And I shall cry if she is hurt.
       —*Daniel J. McGill*

Almighty God and Father of us all,
Have mercy upon this troubled world of ours.
We are a pilgrim people, made of clay,
Captives of our own greed and frailty.
And yet, we are the work of your hands.
You have made us in your own image
And we bear within us
Your Spirit of life,
The seeds of immortality.
Give us, we pray,
A stronger faith
So that we may walk joyously into the unknown,
An unshakable hope
So that we may comfort the despairing,
And a love
As vast as all the oceans
So that we may hold all humankind
In our hearts.
All powerful God,
Look in your love upon us, your pilgrim people,
As we struggle towards you.
Be our food for the journey,
Our wine for rejoicing,
Our light in the darkness,
And our welcome at the journey's end.

—*Sheila Cassidy, England*

*S*ource of all life,
For your name's sake,
For your joy cast upon the Earth,
For life's great delight in your handiwork,
Remember all the wounded and broken things,
    unclean water
    poisoned air
    desecrated land
    fleeing wildlife
    dying innocents
And please remember us,
When our lives become enemies of your life.
Open our hearts to your family,
Earth's many children;
Return our hearts to you. Amen.
    —*Daniel J. McGill*

*M*ake that possible to us, O Lord, by grace,
which appears impossible to us by nature.
    —*Thomas à Kempis, Germany (c. 1380–1471)*

O Come, Thou Dayspring, come and cheer our spirits by Thine advent here; disperse the gloomy clouds of night, and death's dark shadows put to flight.
Rejoice! Rejoice! Immanuel shall come to thee, O Israel!

O come, Desire of nations, bind all peoples in one heart and mind; bid Thou our sad divisions cease; fill the whole world with heaven's peace.
Rejoice! Rejoice! Immanuel shall come to thee, O Israel!

O come, Thou Wisdom from on high, Who ord'rest all things mightily; to us the path of knowledge show and teach us in her ways to go.
Rejoice! Rejoice! Immanuel shall come to thee, O Israel!

—Latin hymn (9th century)

*P*ut your ear to the ground
and listen:
hurried, worried footsteps,
bitterness, rebellion.
Hope
hasn't yet begun.
Listen again.
Put out feelers.
The Lord is there.
He is far less likely
to abandon us
in hardship
than in times of ease.

—Dom Helder Camara, Brazil

A Great Emptiness

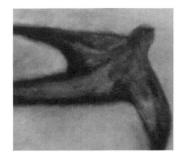

Prayers for
the Healing of Grief

LAMENT PSALM FORTY-EIGHT

1 am depressed, O God.
I see no end to this cycle of sadness.
People tell me: "Everything will be all right,"
but it isn't, and it won't be.
They quote Paul to me:
"All things work together for good for those who love God."
Don't I love you?
Wasn't I brought up in your holy house,
O God?
Didn't I memorize your words and sing hymns to you?
Don't I bow down to you?
Isn't that what I'm doing now?
No one can tell me any good can come from this moment!
Let them have their say if it makes them feel better!
But I don't want to hear it!
I know what I've been through.
I know what it is to have death walk the halls of my home.
What has happened can't be undone.
What is done cannot be prettied up.
But you, O God, can stop the aftershocks.
O God, tear through the night
to rescue the one you have left too long.
Help me, O Holy God,
out of this tomb of pain.
　　　—Ann Weems

*H*ow is faith to endure, O God, when you allow all this scraping and tearing on us? You have allowed rivers of blood to flow, mountains of suffering to pile up, sobs to become humanity's song—all without lifting a finger that we could see. You have allowed bonds of love beyond number to be painfully snapped. If you have not abandoned us, explain yourself.

We strain to hear. But instead of hearing an answer we catch sight of God himself scraped and torn. Through our tears we see the tears of God.

A new and more disturbing question now arises: Why do you permit yourself to suffer, O God? If the death of the devout costs you dear, why do you permit it? Why do you not grasp joy?

—Nicholas Wolterstorff

1 believe in You,
O Holy One,
although at times
there no longer seems
any reason for believing.
When evil stalks
my dwelling place
and loneliness leaves
indelible traces of doubt
on my childhood faith,
I light a lamp
in the secret room
where my heart hides
its tradition
and quietly hug
Your promises
as I sing songs to You.
I believe in You.
Believe in me.
May we believe forever.
Amen.

—Miriam Therese Winter

*T*here's not much to come home to
Now that she's gone.
I keep forgetting,
Sort of expecting her to be there
Like always.
So when I open the door
The silence hits me
Like a fist,
Knocks the wind out of me.
I'm glad there's nobody there to see.
They'd send me up like a kook.
But
The air inside the house is hard and cold
And it used to be warm and soft
With her talking,
Saying nothing,
Asking silly questions—
"Is that you?" she'd ask,
And I'd say, "No, It's Santa Claus,"
Or "the man-in-the-moon,"
But I felt like me
Then.
A lot of the time now I don't.
—*Elise Maclay*

LAMENT PSALM TWENTY-EIGHT

O God, hear me!
I am tormented by the finality of death
and harassed by those who want to explain it . . .
As though the pain of his death is not enough,
their glibness cuts like a razor into my heart
and the bleeding starts again.
O God, have pity on me
and keep them from my doorstep!

Why, O God, do I have to deal with them?
They crouch by my door;
their whispered voices fly in through my window:
"He was in the wrong place at the wrong time!"
O God of my life!
Tell me you were there, too!
Tell me that on your earth there is no wrong place
nor is there any wrong time
for the children of God!
Tell me you caught him in your arms
and wiped the tears from his eyes,
and showed him your face
as you had showed him your heart.
Tell me you are always with us
in life and in death.
Have pity on me, O God,
and keep them from my doorstep!

O God, they're like magpies,
suggesting his death is a test of my faith,
as though you are some egomaniac God
who zaps me from on high,
who demands repeated assurances of my love,
as though you do not know my heart!
Have pity on me, O God, and keep them from my doorstep!
O God, I know you are not what they say!
That you loved him so much that you wanted him
to live in heaven with you!
O God, they blaspheme you and trivialize his death!
I know you, O God of love,
I know you, and your will is life;
your name is compassion.
O God of mercy, send them away!
Let them leave me to my weeping.
Let them leave me with the quiet ones
who sit beside me through the days.
Let them leave me with your word open upon my heart.
Send them away,
but write once more upon their hearts
and upon mine the word of your love.

O merciful God,
there is no trouble I cannot bring to you!
In you only is my trust!
 —Ann Weems

What do I do now with my regrets. When the person is dead, what do we do with our regrets?

. . . I believe that God forgives me. I do not doubt that. The matter between God and me is closed. But . . . my regrets remain. What do I do with my God-forgiven regrets? Maybe some of what I regret doesn't even need forgiving; maybe sometimes I did as well as I could. Full love isn't always possible in this fallen world of ours. Still, I regret.

I shall live with them. I shall accept my regrets as part of my life, to be numbered among my self-inflicted wounds. But I will not endlessly gaze at them. I shall allow the memories to prod me into doing better with those still living. And I shall allow them to sharpen the vision and intensify the hope for that Great Day coming when we can all throw ourselves into each other's arms and say, "I'm sorry."

The God of love will surely grant us such a day. Love needs that.
—*Nicholas Wolterstorff*

"The tears . . . streamed down, and I let them flow as freely as they would, making of them a pillow for my heart. On them it rested."
—*Saint Augustine, North Africa (354–430)*

As the rain hides the stars, as the autumn mist hides the hills, as the clouds veil the blue of the sky, so the dark happenings of my lot hide the shining of your face from me. Yet, if I may hold your hand in the darkness, it is enough. Since I know that, though I may stumble in my going, you do not fall.

—*Gaelic*

1 shall look at the world through tears. Perhaps I shall see things that dry-eyed I could not see.

—*Nicholas Wolterstorff*

Dear Lord, just as you gave us tear ducts to cry, you gave us ribs and stomachs to shake with laughter. My grief is serious work. I have a need for light and lightness in order to keep my balance. Whatever can help me laugh, even as I cry, I will be thankful for. Give me laughter and joy in my grief. In your name I pray. Amen.

—*Philip W. Williams*

*H*er face thins almost
as we watch. Bones
seem larger—grating
on pillow and sheet

like shells on an edge
of shore. We speak

more simply in her presence:
a primer of nouns

and verbs. She lets go
of life gently. We

receive from her hands
the victory of belief,

learning the meaning of
our lives from our grief.
     —*Sister Maura,* S.S.N.D.

*S*he whom we love and lose
is no longer where she was before.
She is now wherever we are.
     —*Saint John Chrysostom, Constantinople (c. 347–407)*

Today I read about a man who slashed his wrists because
   he lost his hat.
He was old, and of course, they say he was crazy.
I think not.
I think he'd just had all the losses he could take.
He said as much.
His last words were, "O God, now I've lost my hat, too."
I know how he felt.
Every time you turn around, time—with a little help from
   your friends—grabs off something else. Something
   precious. At least to you.
Hearing. Sight. Beauty. Job. House. Even the corner grocery
   turns into a parking lot and is lost.
Finally, you lose the thing you can't do without—hope
   (that it can get better).
Dear God, when he gets to heaven, let that man find his
   hat on the gatepost.
   —Elise Maclay

*M*y help is in the mountain
Where I take myself to heal
The earthly wounds
That people give to me.
I find a rock with sun on it
And a stream where the water runs gentle
And the trees which one by one give me company.
So must I stay for a long time
Until I have grown from the rock
And the stream is running through me
And I cannot tell myself from one tall tree.
Then I know that nothing touches me
Nor makes me run away.
My help is in the mountain
That I take away with me.

Earth cure me. Earth receive my woe. Rock
strengthen me. Rock receive my weakness. Rain
wash my sadness away. Rain receive my doubt.
Sun make sweet my song. Sun receive the anger
from my heart.

   —*Nancy Wood, a poetic interpretation of the Taos Pueblo Indian*
      way of seeing and understanding

O God who brought us to birth,
and in whose arms we die:
in our grief and shock
contain and comfort us;
embrace us with your love,
give us hope in our confusion,
and grace to let go into new life,
through Jesus Christ. Amen.
  —*Janet Morley, England*

The Lord bless you and keep you. The Lord make his face shine upon you and be gracious unto you, in your going out and in your coming in, in your rising and in your lying down, in your mourning and in your peace, in your labor and in your leisure, in your laughter and in your tears, until you too come to stand before him in the day to which there is no sunset and no dawn. In the name of the Father, and of the Son and of the Holy Ghost. Amen.
  —*Philip W. Williams*

New Beginnings

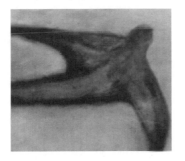

The Healing Power
of Forgiveness

*M*ay God bless us with forgiveness for our sins, reconciliation with those from whom we are divided, and solidarity with all who suffer. Amen.

—*Marchiene Vroon Rienstra*

*L*ord, grant that anger or other bitterness does not reign over us, but that by your grace, genuine kindness, loyalty, and every kind of friendliness, generosity, and gentleness may reign in us. Amen.

—*Martin Luther, Germany (1483–1546)*

*H*oly Presence within me, I am willing to release all feelings of hurt and anger and resentment. Help me know true forgiveness and see each person as part of You. Let my words and my actions serve only to glorify You. May they heal and comfort and harmonize my life and the lives of those around me. Thank You, God.

—*Author unknown*

*H*e makes me so damned angry, Lord. Forgive me. I cannot explain it or justify it and I recognize it as a lack of love and therefore a sin. What am I to do? The minute I see him my nerves stand on edge and when we talk my temper tries at once to break loose from its tenuous moorings. Yet to avoid talking is unkind and cowardly. Give me forbearance I beg you, so that I do not judge or argue with everything he says, but try to understand what he is saying and how I might respond in love.

—*Helen Thomas*

*T*hinking of someone you want to forgive, breathe a simple prayer:

Lord, help me see him/her as you do.

I cannot forgive this person. Please enable me to forgive.

_____, I bless you and release you to the Holy Spirit.

Lord, you have forgiven me. Help me to forgive myself.

*L*ord of creation,
remind all lovers of the power in their marriage.
Tell them of

> the joy, the romance, the fun
> of being man and wife;
> the new places to go,
> new things to do,
> new hopes, new laughter.

Give them

> new touches, new feelings,
> the new gifts, new surprises,
> and new beginnings.

Lord of redemption,
remind all lovers of redemption in marriage.
Tell them of

> the healing, understanding,
> the reconciling, the wiping of tears,
> the dying and rising,
> the fighting and forgiving,
> the kissing and making up,
> the repenting and absolving.

Give them

> the crucifying and the resurrecting,
> the hurting and the healing,
> and the new chance.

Lord of creation and redemption,
have man and woman be Christ to one another. Amen.

—Herbert Brokering

Our Father in heaven, you gave each of your earth children the human power to forgive. We thank you that we are humanly able to forgive each other our mean and hateful acts. But we cannot forgive ourselves, Lord! We cannot forgive our own meanness and hatefulness. We cannot heal the cancer at the marrowbone of our beings.

But even that you have taken care of, Father of us all. In your love for us you have freely forgiven us in your son Jesus Christ, a miracle so amazing that we have not grasped the wonder of it, a condition so brand-new in human history that we do not know how to receive it or to use it.

Oh, teach us, dear Father! Teach us that you are not only a God of forgiveness but that you in very fact and act can accomplish it in us. We pray not for a Sunday sense of forgiveness. We pray not for momentary acts of forgiveness. We pray for the spirit of forgiveness. We pray for the power of will to emigrate from our present state and to move into the new state your son Jesus Christ created for us, the state of forgiveness. We pray that we may become fully naturalized citizens of the state of forgiveness. We pray in your son's name. Amen.

—*Edna Hong*

THE JESUS PRAYER

*L*ord Jesus Christ, Son of God,
have mercy on me, a sinner.

In this prayer, one of the great treasures of the Orthodox church, the
words "have mercy" (*eleison* in Greek) come from the same root as
elaion, olive tree, and the oil from it. So they speak of healing,
soothing, grace.

Each word or phrase in the prayer should be dwelt upon and its
meaning allowed to penetrate through the mind to the heart which
is the center of being.

Lord . . . Jesus . . . Christ . . . Son of God . . .
heal, strengthen, forgive . . . me . . . a sinner

repeated slowly, recollectedly, lovingly . . .
silently, deeply, gratefully.
    —*George Appleton, England (1902–1993)*

*T*oday, O Lord, I accept your acceptance of me.
I confess that you are always with me and always for me.
I receive into my spirit your grace, your mercy, your care.
I rest in your love, O Lord. I rest in your love. Amen.
    —*Richard J. Foster*

*L*ord Jesus, we are silly sheep who have dared to stand before you and try to bribe you with our preposterous portfolios. Suddenly we have come to our senses. We are sorry and ask you to forgive us. Give us the grace to admit we are ragamuffins, to embrace our brokenness, to celebrate your mercy when we are at our weakest, to rely on your mercy no matter what we may do. Dear Jesus, gift us to stop grandstanding and trying to get attention, to do the truth quietly without display, to let the dishonesties in our lives fade away, to accept our limitations, to cling to the gospel of grace, and to delight in your love. Amen.
　　—*Brennan Manning*

*T*he blessing of God,
whose love reconciles all who are divided,
be with you as you seek to heal
the brokenness around you.
　　—*Vienna Cobb Anderson*

I Rest My Soul

Healing and Stillness

*B*e silent.
Be still.
Alone,
Empty
Before your God
Say nothing.
Ask nothing.
Be silent.
Be still.
Let your God
Look upon you.
That is all.
God knows,
Understands,
Loves you with
An enormous love.
God only wants to
Look upon you
With Love.
Quiet.
Still.
Be.

Let your God—
Love you.
        —*Edwina Gateley*

My ego is like a fortress.
I have built its walls stone by stone
To hold out the invasion of the love of God.

But I have stayed here long enough.
There is light over the barriers. O my God—
The darkness of my house forgive
And overtake my soul.
I relax the barriers.
I abandon all that I think I am,
All that I hope to be,
All that I believe I possess.
I let go of the past,
I withdraw my grasping hand from the future,
And in the great silence of this moment,
I alertly rest my soul.
—Howard Thurman (1900–1981)

O you who are at home
Deep in my heart
Enable me to join you
Deep in my heart
—The Talmud

$\mathcal{G}$od, teach me to let my soul rest, to still my worries and doubts,
to stop my constant clatter of questions and protests.
Let me come to you sometimes and just sit quietly,
like a mother smiling at her sleeping baby and listening to its soft
breathing . . .
or like a small child intent on hearing a kitten's purr or a little bird's
chirp . . .
or as if I were trying to hear a soft breeze moving across a pond,
a leaf dropping onto the grass.
Let me learn to wait patiently and trustingly for you
to make things clearer to me.
Teach me to be as calm as a lake after sundown . . .
as trusting as a baby in its mother's lap.
Teach me to grow gradually, unprotestingly, like a flower . . .
to go unresistingly wherever you send me,
like airborne seed obeying the breeze.
Teach me to turn always toward you,
the very essence of love and of life,
the cause of love and life,
the nourisher of love and life,
the purpose of love and life—
the way leaves keep turning toward the life-giving sun.
　　　—*Joan Bel Geddes*

1 thank you that, by the inpouring of your love, you are healing me
of all that is contrary to your Spirit.
　　　—*M. V. Dunlop, England*

Gentle me,
Holy One,
into an unclenched moment
a deep breath,
a letting go
of heavy experiences,
of dead certainties,
that, softened by the silence,
surrounded by the light,
and open to the mystery,
I may be found by wholeness,
upheld by the unfathomable,
entranced by the simple,
and filled with the joy
that is you.
    —*Ted Loder*

Help me now to be quiet, relaxed and receptive, accepting the
thought of healing grace at work, deep within my nature.
    —*Leslie Weatherhead, England (1883–1975)*

O Lord, Jesus Christ, Who art as the Shadow of a Great Rock in a weary land, Who beholdest Thy weak creatures weary of labour, weary of pleasure, weary of hope deferred, weary of self; in Thine abundant compassion, and fellow-feeling with us, and unutterable tenderness, bring us, we pray Thee, unto Thy rest. Amen.

—*Christina Rossetti, England (1830–1894)*

Drop thy still dews of quietness
    Till all our strivings cease;
Take from our souls the strain and stress,
And let our ordered lives confess
    The beauty of thy peace.

Breathe through the heats of our desire
    Thy coolness and thy balm;
Let sense be dumb, let flesh retire;
Speak through the earthquake, wind, and fire,
    O still small voice of calm!

—*John Greenleaf Whittier (1807–1892)*

*S*ay slowly and thoughtfully the first two verses of Psalm 63:
> O God, you are my God:
> early will I seek you.
> My soul thirsts for you, my flesh longs for you:
> in a dry and thirsty land where no water is.

Say it again. Then repeat a few of the key words:
> O God, you are my God . . .
> My soul longs for you . . .

Repeat these phrases several times, until you feel that they are becoming part of you, sinking from your head to your heart like water into a dry plant.
> O God, you are my God
> My soul longs for you . . .

When you are ready, let the prayer become even shorter: My God, or, simply, God.

Let yourself enter into the silence, using the name of God to draw you again and again into the presence, which is beyond words. When distractions come (which they will), offer them to God and then let go of them, returning to the full verse or to the simpler words, so that they can lead you back into silent communion with God. Many passages from the Bible can be prayed over in this way.

—*Angela Ashwin*

*G*rant me the ability to be alone.
May it be my custom to go outdoors each day
among the trees and grasses,
among all growing things
and there may I be alone,
and enter into prayer
to talk with the one
that I belong to.
  —*Rabbi Nachman of Bratzlav, Poland (1772–1811)*

*B*lessèd sister, holy mother,
spirit of the fountain, spirit of the garden,
Suffer us not to mock ourselves with falsehood
Teach us to care and not to care
Teach us to sit still
Even among these rocks,
Our peace in His will
And even among these rocks
Sister, mother
And spirit of the river, spirit of the sea,
Suffer me not be separated

And let my cry come unto Thee.
  —*T. S. Eliot (1888–1965)*

*B*reath Prayers for Stillness:

Lord, come to me, my door is open.

Into your hands I commend my spirit.

Now the silence, now the peace.

Lord, I wait for your healing, your peace, and your Word.

Let not your heart be troubled,
neither let it be afraid.

*A*h, dearest Jesus, holy Child,
Make thee a bed, soft, undefiled,
Within my heart, that it may be
A quiet chamber kept for thee.
  —Martin Luther, Germany (1483–1546)

Those Who Watch

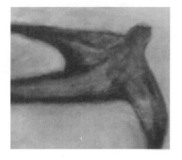

Prayers for
the Healing of Others

Watch, O Lord, with those who wake, or watch,
or weep tonight, and give your angels and saints
charge over those who sleep.
Tend your sick ones, O Lord Christ,
Rest your weary ones,
Bless your dying ones,
Soothe your suffering ones,
Pity your afflicted ones,
Shield your joyous ones,
And all for your love's sake.
   —Saint Augustine, North Africa (354–430)

God of the desert, suffering God, bless this friend who hurts
      and longs for the day when she will be free of distress in mind
      and body.
God of healing and wholeness, fill her empty places with hope
      and embrace her with your comfort and courage.
Like the woman ill for twelve years who touched the hem of
      Jesus' garment, may she touch the garment of your compassion
      and feel spiritual power flow through her body and spirit.
We place our trust in you, God of tender love. Amen.
   —Kathleen Fischer

O Mother and Father of All Things, You whose joy created the Universe, thank you for blessing us with this boy. We place him now in your loving arms. Guide the surgeons' hands; let them find what they must to make possible his healing. We ask nothing for ourselves. We will do whatever is required of us, without complaint, in gratitude for the happiness our children have brought us. We ask only mercy for him. He has suffered so much, and he has so much to give. We beg you, let him live, that he may glorify your Creation. Amen.

—*Phil Catalfo*

*T*hank you Lord. I believe that your power is entering into this person, working toward the wholeness that I see in my mind. Amen.

—*Agnes Sanford (1897–1982)*

*A*t a healing service, when laying on hands, I will often pray: "May the healing love and grace of God be in every corner of your heart, crevice of your mind, and cell of your body."

—*Avery Brooke*

Dear God,
friends with AIDS
slip through my fingers
faster than grains of sand,
and seemingly as many.

I can't hold them.

God, dear God,
please catch them
with your open hands,
within your welcoming embrace,
with your loving heart.

I wish I could be there for them.

I pray they'll be there for me
when I slip.
You too, my God,
our God. Amen.

—Chris Glaser

I lift up my heart, O God, for all who are the prey of anxious fears, who cannot get their minds off themselves and for whom every demand made on them fills them with foreboding, and with the feeling that they cannot cope with all that is required of them.

Give them the comfort of knowing that this feeling is illness, not cowardice; that millions have felt as they feel, that there is a way through this dark valley, and light at the end of it.

Lead them to those who can help them and understand them and show them the pathway to health and happiness. Comfort and sustain them by the loving presence of the Saviour who knows and understands all our woe and fear, and give them enough courage to face each day, and rest their minds in the thought that You will see them through.

—*Leslie Weatherhead, England (1883–1975)*

*W*e remember those who are deep in depression, whose inner world is bleak and dark . . . especially . . .

We remember those who have recently said farewell to a loved one and who feel that joy will never return . . . especially . . .

We remember those who are caught up in running through life and are entangled in frenzied activity . . .

We remember those who struggle to believe in their own goodness . . .

We remember those who have lost their dreams and their enthusiasm for life . . .

We remember those who are experiencing failure in relationships or in work situations . . .

We remember those who doubt their inner growth and who question their journey with God . . .

We remember those who never seem to get beyond financial worries and the pain of caring for the essentials of life . . .

We remember those who have been rejected, deserted, betrayed or abandoned . . .

We remember those who live in the grips of addiction and the throes of self-absorption . . .

We remember those who have lost hope and who daily do battle with thoughts of suicide . . .

We remember those who live constantly with worry and anxiety . . .

—*Joyce Rupp*

$\mathcal{H}$ear my voice, O God, when I groan because I feel so helpless.
Why should one you created suffer so deeply
the disorientation and lostness of a mind confused?
We who know how to make bombs well enough
to blast our planet into oblivion,
why do you not give us the ability
to prevent degenerative disease?
Fragmented, brittle hours of lostness enshroud her day.
Seventy-eight, a flickering candle burning at twilight.
Yet, I remember, there were the good days.
Lark singing overhead
and wild spring flowers in the hedge.
"A pearl," she said, "this day is a pearl,
strung on my necklace of translucent memories."
When she saw mountains for the first time,
"I can't believe it," she cried,
face radiant with gratitude.
We hiked summers away through mist and rain
and walked in winter snow.
It's hard to reach her now as she struggles
in the dark, seeping swamps of confusion.
Like timeless Job I hurl into emptiness
the unanswerable "WHY?"
and in the waiting I remember—
there were the good days.
        —Elizabeth J. Canham

We pray/accept responsibility for children
  who sneak Popsicles before supper,
  who erase holes in math workbooks,
  who can never find their shoes.
And we pray/accept responsibility for those
  who stare at photographers from behind barbed wire,
  who can't bound down the street in a new pair of sneakers,
  who never "counted potatoes,"
  who were born in places we wouldn't be caught dead,
  who never go to the circus,
  who live in an x-rated world.
We pray/accept responsibility for children
  who bring us sticky kisses and fistfuls of dandelions,
  who hug us in a hurry and forget their lunch money.
And we pray/accept responsibility for those
  who never get dessert,
  who have no safe blanket to drag behind them,
  who watch their parents watch them die,
  who can't find any bread to steal,
  who don't have any rooms to clean up,
  whose pictures aren't on anybody's dresser,
  and whose monsters are real.

We pray/accept responsibility for children
    who spend all their allowance before Tuesday,
    who throw tantrums in the grocery store and pick at their food,
    who like ghost stories,
    who shove dirty clothes under the bed
    and never rinse out the tub,
    who get visits from the tooth fairy,
    who don't like to be kissed in front of the carpool,
    who squirm in church or temple and scream in the phone,
    whose tears we sometimes laugh at and whose
        smiles can make us cry.
And we pray/accept responsibility for those
    whose nightmares come in the daytime,
    who will eat anything,
    who have never seen a dentist,
    who aren't spoiled by anybody,
    who go to bed hungry and cry themselves to sleep,
    who live and move, but have no being.
We pray/accept responsibility for children
    who want to be carried and for those who must,
    for those we never give up on and for those
    who don't get a second chance,
    for those we smother and for those who will grab
        the hand of anyone kind enough to offer it.
        —Adapted from Ina J. Hughes

*L*ord,
make more families.
Make them close
that there can be healing and helping
and loving and resting and singing
and eating and drinking
in Your name.
In families
prepare the people for the world.
Send them well loved
into a world in need of much love.
Where there is no father or no mother,
make it a family.
Where there is no family room,
no family album, no uncles and aunts,
let there be a family.
Where there are no birthdays and holidays
and family mealtimes,
bring together enough to make a family.
Make families by love.
May we all belong
somewhere, somehow, to someone.
O Christ, be here in this place
and make it a home.
Amen.
  —Herbert Brokering

May those who doubt
   Trust in their doubt.
May those who cannot believe
   Trust in their disbelief.
May those who are tempted
   Trust their temptation.
May those who are alone
   Trust their aloneness.
May those who are abandoned
   Trust their abandonment.
May those who are desolate
   Trust their desolation.
For by this prayer alone
   All darkness is presented to you, O God.
And as you lead the lost so may you lead them
      by means of that which they do not possess
   To that which they despair ever to find.
May your truth enlighten all paths
   And bring courage in all fears.
      —Daniel J. McGill

1 saw you in the doorway.
You were black and bruised and broken.
I knew you were someone's daughter.

You are your mother's daughter.
If she could, she would sit with you
and say how much she loved you.

I saw you in the shelter.
You looked much older than your years.
Your kids were tired and making a fuss.
I knew you were someone's daughter.

You are your mother's daughter.
Imagine her here, as a sister and friend,
saying how much she loves you.

I saw you on the news last night
on a dirt road in Soweto.
They were screaming at you.
You had no shoes.
I know you were someone's daughter.

You are your mother's daughter
and she is her mother's daughter.
She has put up with so much abuse.
That shows how much she loves you.

I saw you in the delivery room
in drug withdrawal, writhing.
They say you have AIDS. You are three hours old,
and I know you are someone's daughter.

You are your mother's daughter
and she needs you to forgive her.
She doesn't know how to love as yet,
but when she does, I promise you,
she will say how much she loves you.

I saw you in an orphanage.
How sad you looked, and lonely.
they say that you are hard to place,
but I know you are someone's daughter.

You are your mother's daughter
and a foster mother's daughter,
and one of these days, she will come for you
and say how much she loves you.

I saw you in a nursing home.
You were slumped in a chair with a vacant stare.
I knew you were somebody's daughter.

You are your mother's daughter,
your Mother God's own daughter.
Soon, very soon, She will come for you
and say how much She loves you.
—*Miriam Therese Winter*

*L*ord Jesus Christ,

Thou Son of the Most High, Prince of Peace, be born again into our world. Wherever there is war in this world, wherever there is pain, wherever there is loneliness, wherever there is no hope, come, thou long-expected one, with healing in thy wings.

Holy Child, whom the shepherds and the kings and the dumb beasts adored, be born again. Wherever there is boredom, wherever there is fear of failure, wherever there is temptation too strong to resist, wherever there is bitterness of heart, come, thou blessed one, with healing in thy wings.

Saviour, be born in each of us who raises his face to thy face, not knowing fully who he is or who thou art, knowing only that thy love is beyond his knowing and that no other has the power to make him whole. Come, Lord Jesus, to each who longs for thee even though he has forgotten thy name. Come quickly. Amen.
—*Frederick Buechner*

O Lord, this world is full of fear.
Make my fear into a prayer for the fearful.
—*Henri Nouwen (1932–1996)*

*H*olding a name lovingly, trustingly before God,
without diagnosing the person's need,

or telling God what to do,

leaving God to do what in love is
most needed.

The name may be repeated many times,
on the lips or in the mind,
and then, held silently in the heart.

If our Lord's name is added after the name of the
one for whom we are praying,
his love is invoked to magnify our own human love.
   —*George Appleton, England (1902–1993)*

O suffering Christ, lay your hand in healing power upon those
who feel they can bear no more, until their hearts are hushed and
quieted, knowing that round about them and underneath them are
the Everlasting Arms. Amen.
   —*Leslie Weatherhead, England (1883–1975)*

*L*ord, I bring before you
the needs of my parents, friends,
brothers, sisters,
all whom I love,
and all who have asked me to pray for them.
I pray that they may experience your help
and the gift of your comfort,
protection from all dangers,
deliverance from all sin,
and freedom from pain.
May they give you joyful thanks and praise.
I also bring before you
all those who have in any way
offended or insulted me,
or done me any harm.
I also remember those
whom I have hurt or offended or troubled
by what I said or did
knowingly or unknowingly.
Lord, in your mercy, forgive all our sins against one another.
Take from our hearts
all suspicion, hard feelings,
anger, dissension,
and whatever else may diminish the love
we should have for one another.
Have mercy, O Lord, on all who ask your mercy.
Give grace to all who need it,
that we may finally come to eternal life.
　　—Thomas à Kempis, Germany (1380–1471)

*B*reath Prayers for Intercession:

           _____: May the power of God protect you.
May the love of Jesus heal you.
May the wisdom of the spirit guide you.
Now and forever.

Lord Jesus Christ, have mercy on [him, her, them].

Not my will but Yours be done.

Jesus, Healer, make _____ whole.

May _____ be safe from inner and outer enemies.
May _____ be strong and healthy in body.
May _____ be peaceful and calm in mind.
May _____ take care of himself/herself with happy ease.
May _____ come to union with God.

May peace prevail on earth.

*D*ear Lord,
Help me to release my need to control.
Help me to let go and to accept Your will.
I now place this situation lovingly into your hands.
I pray for the highest and the best for all concerned.
Thank you. Amen.
   —*Robert and Janet Ellsworth*

*L*ife, spilling over the hills of our grief
and filling the wells
in our souls and our senses,
come, lift us up into lighthearted laughter,
so all the weight of our awareness
does not overwhelm us.
Life of Our World, be life
in and through us,
now and forever. Amen.
   —*Miriam Therese Winter*

*Y*our heart is good.
The Spirit will be here.
You think only of sad unpleasant things,
You are to think of goodness.
Lie down and sleep here.
Shining darkness will join us.
You think of this goodness in your dream.
Goodness will be given to you,
I will speak for it, and it will come to pass.
It will happen here, I will ask for your good,
It will happen as I sit by you,
It will be done as I sit here in this place.
　　—Yuma Indian Curing Song

*M*ay you face life without illusion,
　　but with gratitude.
Though you have known tragedy,
　　may you nonetheless cherish laughter.
May you have an ever clearer sense of what
　　is important and what is not.
May your encounters with evil
　　heighten your appreciation of what is good.
May you learn to meet death in a way that
　　leads you to celebrate life.
　　—Kathleen Fischer

She is like a horse grazing
a hill pasture that someone makes
smaller by coming every night
to pull the fences in and in.

She has stopped running wide loops,
stopped even the tight circles.
She drops her head to feed; grass
is dust, and the creekbed's dry.

Master, come with your light
halter. Come and bring her in.
  —Jane Kenyon (1947–1995)

Oh Lord who took on human flesh in the person of our Savior
Jesus Christ so that you could walk the last mile to death with each
of us, assist your servant who is now on that last mile. Give her
courage and faith and especially hope that she may face death brave-
ly and teach the rest of us how to die. Bring her home to you where
her life will only just begin, and bring her home as gently as possible. We ask this in the name of Jesus the Lord. Amen.
  —Andrew M. Greeley

Dear Lord, welcome this traveler who has roamed the whole world with an eager and observant eye and a responsive heart. Welcome him as he goes forth now on a new journey to an unknown place.

It is always so hard to say good-bye to someone we love, but we are willing to do so if we know he is embarking on the next stage of fascinating journey and that he is always curious to see things he has never seen before, happy to voyage to places where he has never been before, ready to love appreciatively what he has never known before, and to rejoice in what he loves. So help me to accept the fact that he is parting from me now, traveling far away from me, and help me to hope that we will be rejoined some day.

His journey in recent months has been hard, and he is tired. Comfort him now. And also comfort me, who will miss him so very much, and help me to remember, and to share, and to keep alive his spirit of adventure and love of life. Amen!
—*Joan Bel Geddes*

Receive into Paradise, O Lord,
all those who will sleep tonight
and not awaken again.

Eternal rest give to them, O Lord;
And let perpetual light shine upon them.
—*Traditional Christian Prayer*

Your Grace Has No End

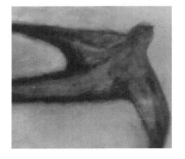

Gratitude for Healings and Blessings

O Lord, Creator,
Ruler of the world, Father,
I thank, thank, thank you
that you have brought me through.
How strong the pain was—
but you were stronger.
How deep the fall was—
but you were even deeper.
How dark was the night—
but you were the noonday sun in it.
You are our father, our mother,
our brother, and our friend.
Your grace has no end,
and your light no snuffer.
We praise you, we honor you,
and we pray to your holy name.
We thank you that you rule thus,
and that you are so merciful
with your tired followers.
    —*Ghana*

May He be blessed forever who has taken such care of me.
May He be blessed forever who has put up with so much from me!
    —*Teresa of Avila, Spain (1515–1582)*

1 suffered, and now there is joy,
I was lonely, and now there is comfort,
I was desolate, and now there is warmth,
I was empty, and now there is fullness.

The years and months of pain dragged on
And plunged me into dark solitude,
And now, why now, do I see the light and feel the warmth?
Is it that my despair reached its depth
And God, in pity, said: Enough?
Where was my soul then
When my spirit was so dead?
And now there is a relief,
An almost tangible gratitude that it is over
And that a spark of life and love
Is being born from nothing.

This will not last forever.
But thank you, God, for living again,
For letting me know and feel
your life and presence in me.
And if this hope should die again,
Let me remember the years of emptiness that passed.
Stay now, God, a little longer.
  —*Edwina Gateley*

$\mathcal{F}$or all the good things I do have and
for all the good things I have had and
for all the good things I will have,
for what I am,
for what I have been,
for what I can be,
for what I shall be,
      thank You, God.
      —Joan Bel Geddes

O God, early in the morning I cry to you.
Help me to pray
And to concentrate my thoughts on you;
I cannot do this alone.
In me there is darkness,
But with you there is light;
I am lonely, but you do not leave me;
I am feeble in heart, but with you there is help;
I am restless, but with you there is peace.
In me there is bitterness, but with you there is patience;
I do not understand your ways,
But you know the way for me.

O heavenly Father,
I praise and thank you
For the peace of the night;
I praise and thank you for this new day;
I praise and thank you for all your goodness
and faithfulness throughout my life.

You have granted me many blessings;
Now let me also accept what is hard
from your hand . . .
You make all things work together for good
for your children.

—*Dietrich Bonhoeffer, Germany (1906–1945)*

*T*he following prayers are intended only as the beginning of a pattern of prayer. You will be able to create your own in a short time. If you pray in this way, you will find your life filled to overflowing with gifts and wonders. Brief blessing prayers are a part of the heritage of every disciple of Jesus, for they were a part of his daily prayer life.

I lift up my heart to you in gratitude
    for this gift of a new day filled with possibilities.
I lift up my heart to you in gratitude, O God,
    for this gift of a hot shower that refreshes me.
I lift up my heart to you in gratitude
    for the gift of this glass of wine
    and its taste of sun, grape and earth.
I lift up my heart to you in gratitude
    for the gift of music
    that delights my ear, my heart and my soul.
I lift up my heart to you in gratitude
    for the ability to read
    and for the wonder of words that speak to my heart.
I lift up my heart to you in gratitude
    for the expression of love I have just shared.
I lift up my heart to you in gratitude
    for the present pain I feel,
    which frames with greater joy the pleasures of my life.
    —Edward Hays

*T*oday is an ordinary day. I thank you, God,
for the ordinary.
I thank you for a day of plain sunlight,
of simple tasks and easy mindless chores.
Sabbath God, I thank you for a day of rest.
No nightmares today.
No new growth today.
No terror today.
I thank you for this ordinary day. Amen.
  —*Catherine J. Foote*

*I*n the godforsaken, obscene quicksand of life,
there is a deafening alleluia
rising from the souls
of those who weep,
and of those who weep with those who weep.
If you watch, you will see
the hand of God
putting the stars back in their skies
one by one.
  —*Ann Weems*

As my mind and heart roam around my life,
I think about, see, hear, feel,
the people who inhabited it—

I think of them gently, now,
how each one blessed me . . . in one way or another.
By who and how they were . . . and are.

Now I bless them
in one way or another
and ask you, my God,
to bless us all.
   —*Marlene Halpin, Dominican*

It is written that "Everywhere, hands lie open to catch us when we
fall." Let us give thanks tonight for this invisible support.
   —*M. J. Ryan*

We give thanks for our friends.
Our dear friends.
We anger each other.
We fail each other.
We share this sad earth, this tender life,
    this precious time.
Such richness. Such wildness.
Together we are blown about.
Together we are dragged along.
All this delight.
All this suffering.
All this forgiving life.
We hold it together. Amen.
    —*Michael Leunig, Australia*

To be joyful in the universe is a brave and reckless act. The courage for joy springs not from the certainty of human experience, but the surprise. Our astonishment at being loved, our bold willingness to love in return—these wonders promise the possibility of joyfulness, no matter how often and how harshly love seems to be lost.

Therefore, despite the world's sorrows, we give thanks for our loves, for our joys and for the continued courage to be happily surprised.
    —*Molly Fumia*

$\mathcal{A}$nd in the evening, when I lie in bed and end my prayers with the words, "I thank you, God, for all that is good and dear and beautiful," I am filled with joy. Then I think about "the good" of going into hiding, of my health and with my whole being of the "dearness" of Peter, of that which is still embryonic and impressionable and which we neither of us dare to name or touch, of that which will come sometime; love, the future, happiness and of "the beauty" which exists in the world; the world, nature, beauty and all, all that is exquisite and fine.

I don't think then of all the misery, but of the beauty that still remains. This is one of the things that Mummy and I are so entirely different about. Her counsel when one feels melancholy is: "Think of all the misery in the world and be thankful that you are not sharing in it!" My advice is: "Go outside, to the fields, enjoy nature and the sunshine, go out and try to recapture happiness in yourself and in God. Think of all the beauty that's still left in and around you and be happy!"

I don't see how Mummy's idea can be right, because then how are you supposed to behave if you go through the misery yourself? Then you are lost. On the contrary, I've found that there is always some beauty left—in nature, sunshine, freedom, in yourself; these can all help you. Look at these things, then you find yourself again, and God, and then you regain your balance.

And whoever is happy will make others happy too. He who has courage and faith will never perish in misery!

—*Anne Frank, Holland (1929–c. 1945)*

*L*ord, I am grateful to You
that in Your mysterious love
You have taken away from me
all earthly wealth,
and that You now clothe and feed me
through the kindness of others.

Lord, I am grateful to You
that since You have taken away from me
the sight of my eyes.
You care for me now
through the eyes of others.

Lord, I am grateful to You
that since you have taken away from me
the strength of my hands and heart,
you care for me now
through the hands and hearts of others.

Lord, I pray for them,
that You will reward them in Your love,
that they may continue to faithfully serve and care
until they come to a happy end
in eternity with You.
    —*Mechthild of Magdeburg, Germany (1210–1280)*

Send Me Someone

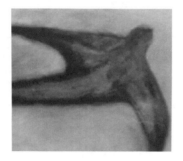

The Healing Power
of Compassion

*H*urting, they came to him,
Healed, they followed him.
Grateful, they gave to him what they had and what they were.
Blessed, they became a blessing
and went out to all the world in his name.

Those who are hurt
and healed
grateful
and blessed
still move among us
in his name.
    —*Ann Weems*

*O*ut of the ashes rises the healer.
    —*Flora Slosson Wuellner*

*L*ord,
when I am famished,
 give me someone who needs food;
when I am thirsty,
 send me someone who needs water;
when I am cold,
 send me someone to warm;
when I am hurting,
 send me someone to console;
when my cross becomes heavy,
 give me another's cross to share;
when I am poor,
 lead someone needy to me;
when I have no time,
 give me someone to help for a moment;
when I am humiliated,
 give me someone to praise;
when I am discouraged,
 send me someone to encourage;
when I need another's understanding,
 give me someone who needs mine;
when I need somebody to take care of me,
 send me someone to care for;
when I think of myself,
 turn my thoughts toward another.
 —*Author unknown, Japan*

*H*aving eaten my last crumb
I hear a voice in the wilderness of my heart.
    Bring me a little water
      the voice pleads.
I am off for the water
when again I am interrupted.
    Bring me a scrap of bread
      the voice calls.
I freeze inside, barely able to believe
      the demands of God.
It is kindness to give someone a drink, yes
But to give out of an empty house is agony.

Someone is asking for a crust of bread
And I have only a few tears
    a handful of flour
    a little oil.
The sticks in my hand are to build a fire,
    to bake a few crumbs for myself
    before I die.

But the call waits in my soul
    like a volcano.
I bake the bread in silence
    with my tears
    with my handful of flour
    with my little oil.
The salt from my tears is the seasoning.
The hungry one eats and is nourished.

Suddenly I am hungry no longer
My vessel of flour is undiminishing
My jar of oil never runs dry.

When you have gathered up the crumbs
    of all you have and are
And baked your bread
    in the only place left:
      the oven of your heart,
Then you will know what it means
    to be bread for the world.
There is a wealth in poverty
    that ought not to be wasted.
There is a nourishment in crumbs
    that ought to be tasted.
    —*Macrina Wiederkehr*

Mother Wisdom Speaks:

Some of you I will hollow out.
I will make you a cave.
I will carve you so deep the stars will shine in your darkness.
You will be a bowl.
You will be the cup in the rock collecting rain.

I will hollow you with knives.
I will not do this to make you clean.
I will not do this to make you pure.
You are clean already.
You are pure already.

I will do this because the world needs the hollowness of you.
I will do this for the space that you will be.
I will do this because you must be large.
A passage.
People will find their way through you.
A bowl.
People will eat from you
and their hunger will not weaken them unto death.
A cup to catch the sacred rain.

My daughter, do not cry. Do not be afraid.
Nothing you need will be lost.
I am shaping you.
I am making you ready.

Light will flow in your hollowing.
You will be filled with light.
Your bones will shine.
The round, open center of you will be radiant.
I will call you Brilliant One.
I will call you Daughter Who Is Wide.
I will call you Transformed.
    —*Christine Lore Webber*

*J*esus, you cared for all the sick who came to you. I want to care
with loving compassion, to attend to details with gentleness. But I
become weary and impatient, angry and abrupt. It is hard to watch
the suffering of someone I love, hard to find energy for all I must do.
I grow discouraged and resentful. Let me learn from your life of
compassion.

Spirit of healing and comfort, be with me in these difficult times.
Teach me to take time for myself, to be gentle with my own limits,
to ask for help from others. May your grace allow me to forgive
myself when I fail, to let go of my expectations, to grieve all my
losses. Send your healing power to me and the one for whom I care.
We trust in your love.
    —*Kathleen Fischer*

*M*ay the pain of our loss
—Increase the fire of our love
May the pain of our guilt
—Ignite the flame of mercy in us
May the pain of our mistakes
—Light for us the path to wisdom
May the pain of our hatreds
—Awaken us to compassion
May the pain of our limitations
—Enkindle in us understanding
May the pain of our regrets
—Shine forth in forgiveness.
—*Daniel J. McGill*

*U*nbidden came Gods love,
not rushing from the skies
as angel, flame or dove
but shining through your eyes.
—*Thomas H. Troeger*

*G*od, help us to enter into the troubles of others, know them as if they were our own, and act accordingly.
   —*Avery Brooke*

*G*ive me, Lord, a stout heart to bear my own burdens, a tender heart to bear the burdens of others and a believing heart to lay all my burdens on you, for you care for us.
   —*Lesslie Newbigin*

*P*ray for one another, so that you may be healed.
   —*James 5:16*

*Y*ou may call God love
you may call God goodness.
But the best name for God is compassion.
   —*Meister Eckhart, Germany (c. 1260–c. 1328)*

Into Your Hands

Facing Death

Into Your Hands, O God,
This solitude,
Into Your Hands, O God,
This emptiness.
Into Your Hands, O God,
This loneliness,
Into Your Hands—
This all.
Into Your Hands, O God,
This grief,
Into Your Hands
This sleeping fear.

Into Your Hands, O God—
What is left,
What is left
Of me.
   —*Edwina Gateley*

I have always known
That at last I would
Take this road,
but yesterday
I did not know
it would be today.
   —*Author unknown, Japan*

Always, before this, I've just been sick for a while, a few days or a week or so. Once it was a matter of months. But now I realize that I may not get well. I may have to live with this pain until I die and come to you.

I don't want to face that, God. Neither pain that doesn't go away, nor death. I know that they come to us all, but I am not ready—not anywhere near ready.

Help me, God. Give me the hope, the patience and the courage that I need. Help me not to be too envious of those who are well. Take away my anger and resentment so that I don't hurt those around me. Help me to use my reduced energies and opportunities to the best of my ability. And above all, give me greater love and understanding for my family, my friends, and all those I see from day to day.
—*Avery Brooke*

Let us live in such a way
That when we die
Our love will survive
And continue to grow. Amen.
—*Michael Leunig, Australia*

*T*he word of death
curves around my heart
like a question mark
whispers
who are you really
what do you care about
what do you really want
what matters
The word of death
presses its way quietly,
insistently into my mind
reminding me
there's no time to waste
in choosing love
this day is precious,
this moment—this one—
is all we have
why wait
why leave unspoken now
a single word
that love would speak
why leave undone
a single gesture
love would express
what could possibly matter more
than love now
than peace now
than forgiveness and freedom now

what foolish reasons
or excuses of fear
do not pale next to the truth
that love is here
that now is all there is eternally
How can I choose less
than to love
with all of my heart, mind, and soul
you
and life
and everything
now

The word of death
comes into my life
bearing a sacred promise
and gift—
calls me to awaken today to life
and the truth of love
as all that matters
and is
and lives.
   —*Diane Berke*

O Lord God,
great distress has come upon me;
my cares threaten to crush me,
and I do not know what to do.
O God, be gracious to me and help me.
Give me strength to bear what you send,
and do not let fear rule over me;
Take a father's care of my wife and children.

O merciful God,
forgive me all the sins that I have committed
against you and against my fellow men.
I trust in your grace
and commit my life wholly into your hands.
Do with me according to your will
and as is best for me.
Whether I live or die, I am with you,
and you, my God, are with me.
Lord, I wait for your salvation
and for your kingdom. Amen.
   —Dietrich Bonhoeffer, Germany (1906–1945)

$\mathcal{F}$ather, my Father! All things are possible for you.
Take this cup of suffering away from me.
Yet not what I want, but what you want.
   —From Mark 14, Jesus' prayer in Gethsemane

I worry and I wish.
I wish I had taken care of more things
    before I got this sick.
I worry what will happen to them
    if I don't recover.
I think maybe tomorrow
I'll have the strength
to do something about it.

I know probably I won't.

Help me to be at peace
with all the things
that are left undone,
my God.
    —*Marlene Halpin, Dominican*

*G*o into the light
and do not look back.
We will care for everything here.
    —*Cheyenne Native American*

*L*ord, I am ill and I don't know what is wrong with me and no one will tell me. Help me for I am afraid of dying; afraid that I will cease to be and that the world will go on as if I had never been. After the fullness and joyfulness of living, this is a terrifying thought. Lord I am no longer sure that I believe you exist, or, if you do, that you love and care for me; yet I think I have experienced your love, come to know you in prayer. But here I am back with my childhood fear of ending in nothing. Please give me a firmer belief and a deeper knowledge of you so that I may trust that when I die I will come to live more fully with you than I have ever done here.
　　—*Michael Hollings and Etta Gullick*

*L*ord,
If I have to die
Let me die;
But please,
Take away this fear.
　　—*Ken Walsh*

$\mathcal{P}$ain isolates,
No matter how many friends you have
Or how devoted.
Well-meaning, they sit beside your bed,
And press your hands,
You slip away,
Though your fingers stay entwined.
I have gone into the pain, deep and far,
How cold, how desolate it is here,
Starting at every sound,
Half hoping, half in fear,
Death, is that you?
Now, are you here?
    —Elise Maclay

$\mathcal{M}$y boat is very small,
Heavily laden with stones:
The waves run high around,
The stream is wide, and very swift:
Take thou the helm, my God,
Oh let thy mercy steer her on,
And bring her to the farther shore in peace.
    —Giridhar, India (17th century)

O Lord, I've turned my eyes and my prayers to you so very often. There have been times when I've felt forgotten by you and I really wondered if you were still there to hear me. Times when I got so discouraged I prayed to die. Times when I was so broken and depressed I didn't feel like talking to anyone. Times when I was so angry I felt like screaming and crying at the same time. Times when I felt so helpless, so hopeless I didn't even want to try again. I have hoped so many times, bargained and prayed in so many ways.

O Lord, as you hear my cry and see my tears, I pray that you may give me that peace of mind which comes from leaving things up to you. Help me to live one day at a time, to find new strength in you as my body weakens, to be grateful for all that is done to take away the pain and make me comfortable. Stay by my side as I walk through the dark valley so that your light may lead me to your undiscovered mountain. I ask this in Jesus' name. Amen.

—*Father Arnaldo Pangrazzi*

*H*ow to make these last days count, God? To live them with courage, and without complaint. To give and receive small joys. To teach the best already learned and to learn a little more.

—*Avery Brooke*

LET EVENING COME

*L*et the light of late afternoon
shine through chinks in the barn, moving
up the bales as the sun moves down.

Let the cricket take up chafing
as a woman takes up her needles
and her yarn. Let evening come.

Let dew collect on the hoe abandoned
in long grass. Let the stars appear
and the moon disclose her silver horn.

Let the fox go back to its sandy den.
Let the wind die down. Let the shed
go black inside. Let evening come.

To the bottle in the ditch, to the scoop
in the oats, to air in the lung
let evening come.

Let it come, as it will, and don't
be afraid. God does not leave us
comfortless, so let evening come.
    —*Jane Kenyon (1947–1995)*

Remain with us, Lord
for evening approaches
and daylight dwindles.
Remain with us
and with your entire Church.
Remain with us
as daylight dwindles,
as our lives dwindle,
at the end of the world.

Remain with us,
through your grace and kindness,
through your sacred Word and
     sacrament,
through your help and benediction.

Remain with us
when we are visited
by nighttime's torment and anguish,
nighttime's doubts and temptations,
the painful nighttime of death.

Remain with us and all the faithful
world without end. Amen.
     —*Wilhelm Löhe, Bavaria (1808–1872)*

Abide with me, fast falls the eventide;
The darkness deepens; Lord, with me abide:
When other helpers fail, and comforts flee;
Help of the helpless, O abide with me.

Swift to its close ebbs out life's little day;
Earth's joys grow dim, its glories pass away;
Change and decay in all around I see;
O Thou who changest not, abide with me.

I need Thy presence every passing hour;
What but Thy grace can foil the tempter's power?
Who like Thyself my guide and stay can be?
Through cloud and sunshine, O abide with me.

I fear no foe, with Thee at hand to bless;
Ills have no weight, and tears no bitterness:
Where is death's sting? Where, grave, thy victory?
I triumph still, if Thou abide with me.

Hold Thou Thy cross before my closing eyes;
Shine through the gloom and point me to the skies;
Heaven's morning breaks, and earth's vain shadows flee;
In life, in death, O Lord, abide with me.
  —*Henry Francis Lyte, England (1793–1847)*

O Lord, support us all the day long of this troublous life, until the shadows lengthen and the evening comes, and the busy world is hushed, and the fever of life is over, and our work is done. Then in Thy mercy grant us a safe lodging, and a holy rest, and peace at the last. Through Jesus Christ our Lord. Amen.

—*John Henry Newman, England (1801–1890)*

*A*s Thou wast before
At my life's beginning,
Be Thou so again
    At my journey's end.

As Thou wast besides
At my soul's shaping,
Father, be Thou too
    At my journey's close.

Be with me a-watching
Each evening and morning,
And allure me home
    To the land of the saints.
    —*Carmina Gadelica, Volume III*

O God, you who in your love have kept me vigorously and joyfully at work in days gone by, and now send me joyful and contented into silence and inactivity, grant that I may find happiness in you in all my solitary and quiet hours. In your strength, O God, I bid farewell to all. The past you know: I leave it at your feet. Grant me grace to respond to your divine call, to leave all that is dear on earth, and to go out alone to you. Behold, I come quickly, says the Lord. Come, Lord Jesus.

 —*Prayer of a priest in old age, India*

Wild Nights—Wild Nights!
Were I with thee
Wild Nights should be
Our luxury!

Futile—the Winds—
To a Heart in port—
Done with the Compass—
Done with the Chart!

Rowing in Eden—
Ah, the Sea!
Might I but moor—Tonight—
In Thee!

 —*Emily Dickinson (1830–1886)*

$\mathcal{P}$recious Lord, take my hand,
Lead me on, let me stand.
I am tired, I am weak, I am worn.

Through the storm, through the night,
Lead me on to the light.
Take my hand, Precious Lord, lead me home.

When my way grows drear, Precious Lord, linger near
When my life is almost gone.
Hear my cry, hear my call, hold my hand, lest I fall.
Take my hand, Precious Lord, lead me home.

When the darkness appears and the night draws near
And the day is past and gone,
At the river I stand,
Guide my feet, hold my hand.
Take my hand, Precious Lord, lead me home.
  —*Thomas A. Dorsey (1899–1993)*

O Comforter of priceless worth
Send peace and unity on earth;
Support us in our final strife
And lead us out of death to life.
  —*Martin Luther, Germany (1483–1546)*

*T*oday is a very good day to die.
Every living thing is in harmony with me.
Every voice sings a chorus within me.
All beauty has come to rest in my eyes.
All bad thoughts have departed from me.
Today is a very good day to die.
My land is peaceful around me.
My fields have been turned for the last time.
My house is filled with laughter.
My children have come home.
Yes, today is a very good day to die.
    —*Nancy Wood*

*T*hink of—
Stepping on shore, and finding it Heaven!
Of taking hold of a hand, and finding it God's hand,
Of breathing new air, and finding it celestial air,
Of feeling invigorated, and finding it immortality,
Of passing from storm and tempest to an unbroken calm,
Of waking up, and finding it Home.
    —*Author unknown*

*B*e each saint in heaven,
Each sainted woman in heaven,
Each angel in heaven
Stretching their arms for you,
Smoothing the way for you,
when you go thither
Over the river hard to see;
Oh when you go thither home
Over the river hard to see.
—*Carmina Gadelica, Volume III*

O Lord, you have made us very small, and we bring our years to an end, like a tale that is told. Help us to remember that beyond our brief day is the eternity of your love.
—*Reinhold Niebuhr (1892–1971)*

$\mathcal{M}$ay my homeland continue to live beyond my life.

    Amen.

May children continue to live in my homeland many generations.

    Amen.

May it be blessed with abundance and health in its air, its water and its soil.

    Amen.

May the wild creatures it has borne bear many descendants and may they not be driven from their homes.

    Amen.

May the plants it gives life to, no matter how humble, prosper a thousand generations.

    Amen.

May every creature there dwelling, especially humans, love my homeland, for she is our mother.

    Amen.

    —Daniel J. McGill

*L*ong before we were born or our mothers and fathers were born or their mothers and fathers were born, you were.

Before there were any people or any world you were here.

And you made us with love and watched us and picked us up when we fell and helped us try again. And all our lives you will love us and when we leave the world we will come home to you. And our children and our children's children will love you, and come home to you. And your kingdom will always wait for us and for all the people who ever were or ever will be.
—*Avery Brooke*

*A*ll shall be Amen and Alleluia.
We shall rest and we shall see,
We shall see and we shall know.
We shall know and we shall love.
We shall love and we shall praise.
Behold our end which is no end.
—*Saint Augustine, North Africa (354–430)*

O God, our help in ages past,
  Our hope for years to come,
Our shelter from the stormy blast,
  And our eternal home.

Under the shadow of thy throne
  Thy saints have dwelt secure;
Sufficient is thine arm alone,
  And our defence is sure.

Before the hills in order stood,
  Or earth receiv'd her frame,
From everlasting thou art God,
  To endless years the same.

A thousand ages in thy sight
  Are like an evening gone;
Short as the watch that ends the night
  Before the rising sun.

Our God, our help in ages past,
  Our hope for years to come,
Be thou our guard while troubles last,
  And our eternal home.
    —Isaac Watts, England (1674–1748)

1 am Resurrection and I am Life, says the Lord.
Whoever has faith in me shall have life,
even though he die.
And everyone who has life,
and has committed himself to me in faith,
shall not die for ever.

As for me, I know that my Redeemer lives
and that at the last he will stand upon the earth.
After my awaking, he will raise me up;
and in my body I shall see God.
I myself shall see, and my eyes behold him
who is my friend and not a stranger.

For none of us has life in himself,
and none becomes his own master when he dies.
For if we have life, we are alive in the Lord,
and if we die, we die in the Lord.
So, then, whether we live or die,
we are the Lord's possession.

Happy from now on
are those who die in the Lord!
So it is, says the Spirit,
for they rest from their labors.
    —*Book of Common Prayer*

Acknowledgments

The editor gratefully acknowledges the following sources for their contributions to this collection. Any omissions are unintentional and will be corrected upon future printings.

Let Comfort Come—Prayers for Physical Healing

Page 12: "Almighty God you are the source," from *Healing in the Landscape of Prayer*. Copyright © 1996 Avery Brooke. Used by permission of Cowley Publications.

Page 12: "Merciful God, Loving Mother," from *Forty Nights: Creation Centered Night Prayer* by Daniel J. McGill. Copyright © 1993 Daniel J. McGill. Used by permission of Paulist Press.

Page 13: "Just for today, what does it matter," Saint Therese of Lisieux, France. (1873–1897).

Page 13: "From moment to moment," Teresa of Avila, Spain. (1515–1582).

Page 14: "My God—equally present," from *Psalms of a Laywoman* by Edwina Gateley. Used by permission of the author.

Page 14: "Help me to be brave," from *To Barbara with Love* by Joan Bel Geddes. Copyright © 1974 Holub & Assoc. Used by permission.

Page 15: "Praying a Bible Text," from *Jerusalem Prayers for the World Today* by George Appleton. Copyright © 1974 George Appleton. Used by permission of Miss M. Appleton.

Page 16: "Jesus, you wasted no time agonizing," from *Turn Over Any Stone* by Edna Hong. Copyright © 1970 Augsburg Publishing House. Used by permission of Postcript, Inc.

Page 17: "Some people find the imagination a useful tool," from *Prayer Without Pretending* by Angela Ashwin. Copyright © 1991 Angela Ashwin. Used by permission.

Page 18: "I experienced it again today," from *Greater Than Our Hearts: Prayers and Reflections* by Ulrich Schaffer. Copyright © 1981 Ulrich Schaffer. Used by permission of HarperCollins Publishers.

Page 18: "We cannot fall beneath the arms of God," William Penn. (1644–1718).

Page 19: "Dear God, the pain of this life is more than I can bear," from *Illuminata* by Marianne Williamson. Copyright © 1994 by Marianne Williamson. Used by permission of Random House.

Page 19: "Jesus Christ, if you had not cried," Thomas R. Heath, O.P.

The Burdens We Carry—Prayers for Mental and Emotional Healing

Page 32: "God of our life, there are days," Saint Augustine of Hippo. (354–430).

Page 33: "I am, O God, a jumbled mass of motives," from *Prayers from the Heart* by Richard J. Foster. Copyright © 1994 Richard J. Foster. Used by permission of HarperCollins Publishers.

Page 33: "O God, Giver of Life," from *Celebrating Women* by H. Ward, J. Wild, and J. Morley. Copyright © 1995 Janet Morley. Used by permission of Christian Aid and Morehouse Publishing.

Page 34: "I keep projecting my present condition," from *A Cry for Mercy* by Henri J.M. Nouwen. Copyright © 1981 by Henri J.M. Nouwen. Used by permission of Doubleday, a division of Bantam Doubleday Dell Publishing Group.

Page 35: "O Love unspeakable and full of glory," from *Best Loved Hymns and Prayers of the American People,* edited by Harold V. Milligan. (Halcyon House, 1942).

Page 35: "Give me a candle of the spirit," from *Jerusalem Prayers for the World Today* by George Appleton. Copyright © 1974 George Appleton. Used by permission of Miss M. Appleton.

Page 36: "I carry the sorrows of my years," from *Time To Become Myself: Reflections on Growing Older* by Pat Corrick Hinton. Copyright © 1990 Pat Corrick Hinton. Used by permission of the author.

Page 36: "Now you too may kneel before the Christ child," from *The Secret of the Gifts* by Paul Flucke. Used by permission of the author.

Page 37: "This life is not a state of being righteous," from *Daily Readings with Martin Luther,* edited by James Atkinson. Copyright © 1987 Templegate Publishers. Used by permission.

Page 37: "Holy Spirit, giving life to all life," Hildegard of Bingen; from *The Enlightened Heart,* translated by Stephen Mitchell. Copyright © 1989 Stephen Mitchell. Used by permission of HarperCollins Publishers.

Page 38: "When I was small," from *Survivor Prayers: Talking with God about Childhood Sexual Abuse* by Catherine J. Foote. Copyright © 1994 Catherine J. Foote. Used by permission of Wesminster John Knox Press.

Page 39: "Dear God, I feel such pain, anxiety, and depression," from *Illuminata* by Marianne Williamson. Copyright © 1994 by Marrianne Williamson. Used by permission of Random House.

Page 39: "I was terrified I'd break down," Rosalind M. Baker from *Quaker Faith and Practice, Book of Christian Discipline of the Yearly Meeting of the Religious Society of Friends (Quakers) in Britian.* (Warwick Printing, 1995).

Page 40: "Dear Higher Power, show me the miracle," from *The Caregiver's Journal,* Vol. 12, No. 3. Copyright © 1996 College of Chaplains. Used by permission.

Thy Kingdom Come—Prayers for the Healing of Community

Page 52: Matthew 6:10

Page 52: "O Lord, whose power to heal," from *Prayers for Today's Church* edited by R. H. L Williams. Copyright © 1977 R. H. L. Williams. Administered and used by permission of Augsburg Fortress.

Page 53: "Bless your people, Lord," from *National Council of Churches of the Philippines, 14th Biennial Convention Resource Book,* 1989.

Page 53: "Lord Jesus, you were awakened by the cry of your disciples," Author unknown.

Page 54: "Lord Jesus Christ, help us not to fall," from *The Hungering Dark* by Frederick Buechner. Copyright © 1969 Frederick Buechner. Used by permission of HarperCollins Publishers.

Page 54: "From the mingled light," from *Hoping Against All Hope* by Dom Helder Camara. Original text copyright © 1981 Pendo Verlag AG, Zurich. English translation copyright © Orbis Books. Used by permission of the publishers.

Page 55: "All the broken hearts shall rejoice," from *In God's Image,* April 1986. Copyright © Asian Women's Resource Center. Used by permission.

Page 55: Psalm 126

Pages 56–57: "I believe that God has the whole world," from *Sharing the Darkness* by Sheila Cassidy. Published and copyright © 1988 Darton, Longman and Todd and 1991 by Orbis Books. Used by permission of the publishers.

Page 57: "God of all good life," from *A Lenten Prayer* by Obie Wright Jr. Copyright © 1994 Personal Papers of Obie Wright Jr., Olney, MD.

Page 58: "O Lord, once I was smart enough," Lewis B. Smedes from *Peace Prayers.* Copyright © Lewis B. Smedes. Used by permission.

Page 58: "Lead me from death to life," adapted from the Upanishads.

Page 58: "Goodness is stronger than evil," from *An African Prayer Book* selected by Desmond Tutu. Copyright © 1995 by Desmond Tutu. Used by permission of Doubleday, a division of Bantam Doubleday Dell Publishing Group.

Page 59: "Bless, O God, my enemies with sunshine," from *Forty Nights: Creation Centered Night Prayer* by Daniel McGill. Copyright © 1993 Daniel J. McGill. Used by permission of Paulist Press.

Page 60: "Almighty God and Father of us all," from *Prayer For Pilgrims: A Book About Ordinary People* by Sheila Cassidy. Copyright © 1980, 1994 HarperCollins Religious Publishers, UK. Used by permission.

Page 61: "Source of all life, for your name's sake," from *Forty Nights: Creation Centered Night Prayer* by Daniel J. McGill. Copyright ©1993 Daniel J. McGill. Used by permission of Paulist Press.

Page 61: "Make that possible to us," Thomas à Kempis. (*c.* 1380–1471).

A Great Emptiness—Prayers For The Healing of Grief

New Beginnings—The Healing Power of Forgiveness

Page 80: "May God bless us with forgiveness," from *Swallows Nest: A Feminine Reading of the Psalms* by Marchiene Vroon Rienstra. Copyright © 1992 William B. Eerdmans Publishing. Used by permission.

Page 80: "Lord, grant that anger or other bitterrness," from *Luther's Works: American Edition* edited by Jaroslav Pelikan and Helmut Lehman. Copyright © 1955 Fortress Press and Concordia Publishing House. Used by permission.

Page 80: "Holy Presence within me," Author unknown.

Page 81: "He makes me so damned angry," from *Personal Prayers* by Helen Thomas. Copyright © 1978 Arena Lettres. Used by permission of Ashgate Publishing.

Page 81: "I cannot forgive," Corrie Ten Boom, Holland.

Page 81: "_____, I bless you," Marianne Williamson.

Page 82: "Lord of creation, remind all lovers," from *Lord Be With* by Herbert Brokering. Copyright © Herbert Brokering. Used by permission.

Page 83: "Our Father in Heaven, you gave each," from *Forgiveness Is a Work Is Well As a Grace* by Edna Hong. Copyright © 1983 Edna Hong. Used by permission of Postscript, Inc.

Page 84: "The Jesus Prayer," from *Jerusalem Prayers for the World Today* by George Appleton. Copyright © 1974 George Appleton. Used by permission of Miss M. Appleton.

Page 84: "Today, O Lord, I accept," from *Prayers from the Heart* by Richard J. Foster. Copyright © 1994 Richard J. Foster. Used by permission of HarperCollins Publishers.

Page 85: "Lord Jesus, we are silly sheep," from *Reaching the Heart of Your Teen* by Gary and Anne Marie Ezzo. Copyright © 1997 by Gary and Anne Marie Ezzo. Used by permission of Multnomah Publishers.

Page 85: "The blessing of God whose love reconciles," from *Prayers of Our Hearts: In Word and Action* by Vienna Cobb Anderson. Copyright © Vienna Cobb Anderson. Used by permission of Crossroad Publishing Company.

I Rest My Soul—Healing and Stillness

Page 88: "Be silent. Be still," from *There Was No Path So I Trod One* by Edwina Gateley. Copyright © Edwina Gateley. Used by permission of the author.

Page 89: "My Ego Is Like a Fortress," from *Deep As the Hunger* by Howard Thurman. (1900–1981). Copyright © Howard Thurman. Used by permission of Friends United Press.

Page 89: "O you who are at home," The Talmud.

Page 90: "God, teach me to let my soul rest," from *To Barbara With Love* by Joan Bel Geddes. Copyright © Joan Bel Geddes. Administered and used by permission of Holub & Associates.

Page 90: "I thank you," from *A Private House of Prayer* by Leslie Weatherhead. Copyright © Leslie Weatherhead. Administered and used by permission of William Neill-Hall.

Page 91: "Gentle me, Holy one," from *Guerrillas of Grace: Prayers for the Battle* by Ted Loder. Copyright © 1984. Used by permission of Innisfree Press, Philadelphia, PA.

Page 91: "Help me now to be quiet," from *A Private House of Prayer* by Leslie Weatherhead. Copyright © Leslie Weatherhead. Administered and used by permission of William Neill-Hall.

Page 92: "O Lord, Jesus Christ, Who art as the Shadow," Christina Rosetti. (1830–1894).

Page 92: "Drop thy still dews of quietness," John Greenleaf Whittier. (1807–1892).

Page 93: "Say slowly and thoughtfully," from *Prayer Without Pretending* by Angela Ashwin. Copyright © 1991 Angela Ashwin. Used by permission.

Page 94: "Grant me the ability to be alone," Rabbi Nachman of Bratslav. (1772–1811).

Page 94: "Blessèd sister, holy mother," excerpted from "Ash Wednesday" in *Collected Poems 1909–1962*, copyright © 1930 by T.S. Eliot and renewed 1971 by Esme Valerie Eliot, reprinted by permission of Harcourt Brace & Company and Faber and Faber.

Page 95: "Lord Come to me," Michel Quoist.

Page 95: "Now the silence," Jaroslav Vajda.

Page 95: "Lord, I wait for your healing," George Appleton. (1902–1993).

Page 95: "Ah, dearest Jesus, holy child," Martin Luther. (1483–1546).

Those Who Watch—Prayers For the Healing of Others

Page 98: "Watch, O Lord, with those who wake," Saint Augustine of Hippo. (354–430).

Page 98: "God of the desert," *Autumn Gospel: Women in the Second Half of Life* by Kathleen Fischer. Copyright © 1995 Kathleen Fischer. Used by permission of Paulist Press.

Page 99: "O Mother and Father of All things," from *Raising Spiritual Children in a Material World*. Copyright © 1997 Phil Catalfo. Permission granted by The Berkely Publishing Group, a division of Penguin Putnam.

Page 99: "Thank you Lord. I believe," from *The Healing Power of the Bible* by Agnes Sanford. Copyright © 1969 by Agnes Sanford. Used by permission of HarperCollins Publishers.

Page 99: "At a healing service," from *Healing In the Landscape of Prayer*. Copyright © 1996 Avery Brooke. Used by permission of Cowley Publications.

Page 100: "Dear God, friends with AIDS," from *Coming Out to God: Prayers for Lesbians and Gay Men, Their Families, and Friends.* Copyright © 1991 Chris Glaser. Used by permission of Westminster John Knox Press.

Page 101: "I lift up my heart," from *A Private House of Prayer* by Leslie Weatherhead. Copyright © Leslie Weatherhead. Administered and used by permission of William Neill-Hall.

Page 116: "In the Nursing Home," from *Otherwise: New and Selected Poems* by Jane Kenyon. Copyright © 1996 Estate of Jane Kenyon. Used by permission of Graywolf Press, St. Paul, MN.

Page 116: "Oh Lord who took on human flesh," from *A Book of Irish American Blessings and Prayers.* Copyright © 1991 Andrew M. Greeley. Used by permission of Thomas More Publishers.

Page 117: "Dear Lord, welcome this traveler," from *To Barbara With Love* by Joan Bel Geddes. Copyright © Joan Bel Geddes. Administered and used by permission of Holub & Associates.

Page 117: "Receive into Paradise," Traditional Christian Prayer.

Your Grace Has No End—Gratitude for Healings and Blessings

Page 120: "O Lord, Creator, Ruler of the World," from *Morning, Noon and Night* edited by John Carden. Copyright © 1976 Church Missionary Society. Used by permission.

Page 120: "May he be blessed forever," Teresa of Avila. (1515–1582).

Page 121: "I suffered and now there is joy," from *Psalms of a Laywoman* by Edwina Gateley. Copyright © Edwina Gateley. Used by permission.

Page 122: "For all the good things I do have," from *To Barbara With Love* by Joan Bel Geddes. Copyright © Joan Bel Geddes. Administered and used by permission of Holub & Associates.

Page 123: "O God, early in the morning I cry," from *Prayers from Prison* by Dietrich Bonhoeffer. Copyright © 1978 Fortress Press. Used by permission.

Page 124: "I lift up my heart to you in gratitude," from *Prayers for a Planetary Pilgrim* by Edward Hays. Copyright © Forest of Peace Publishing House. Used by permission.

Page 125: "Today is an ordinary day," from *Survivor Prayers* by Catherine J. Foote. Copyright © 1994 Catherine J. Foote. Used by permission of Westminster John Knox Press.

Page 125: "In the godforsaken, obscene quicksand of life," from *Psalms of Lament* by Ann Weems. Copyright © 1995 Ann Weems. Used by permission of Westminster John Knox Press.

Page 126: "As my mind and heart roam," from *Right Side Up! Reflections for Those Living With Serious Illness* by Marlene Halpin. Copyright © 1995 Marlene Halpin. Used by permission of Islewest Publishing.

Page 126: "It is written," from *A Grateful Heart* by M. J. Ryan. Copyright © 1994 M.J. Ryan. Used by permission of Conari Press.

Page 127: "We give thanks for our friends," from *The Prayer Tree* by Michael Leunig. Copyright © 1973 Michael Leunig. Used by permission of HarperCollins, Australia.

Page 127: "To be joyful in the universe is a brave and reckless act," from *A Grateful Heart* by M.J. Ryan. Copyright © 1994 by Molly Fumia. Used by permission of Conari Press.

Page 128: "And in the evening when I lie in bed," from *The Works of Anne Frank* by Anne Frank. Copyright © 1952, 1959 Otto H. Frank. Used by permission of Doubleday, a division of Bantam Doubleday Dell Publishing Group and the Heinemann Group.

Page 129: "Lord, I am grateful to You," from *The Little Book of Prayers* by David Schiller. Copyright © 1996 David Schiller. Used by permission of Workman Publishing, New York.

Send Me Someone—The Healing Power of Compassion

Page 132: "Hurting, they came to him," from *Kneeling In Jerusalem* by Ann Weems. Copyright © 1992 Oscar Cullman. Used by permission of Westminster John Knox Press.

Page 132: "Out of the ashes rises the healer," from *Heart of Healing, Heart of Light* by Flora Slosson Wuellner. Copyright © 1992 Flora Slosson Wuellner. Used by permission of Upper Room Books.

Page 133: "Lord, when I am famished," Author unknown.

Pages 134–135: "Having eaten my last crumb," from *A Tree Full of Angels* by Macrina Wiederkehr. Copyright © 1988 Macrina Wiederkehr. Used by permission of HarperCollins Publishers.

Pages 136–137: "Some of you I will hollow out," from *Circle of Mysteries: The Women's Rosary Book* by Christine Lore Webber. Copyright © 1997 Yes International Publishers. Used by permission.

Page 137: "Jesus, you cared for all the sick," from *Autumn Gospel* by Kathleen Fischer. Copyright © 1995 Kathleen Fischer. Used by permission of Paulist Press.

Page 138: "May the pain of our loss," from *Forty Nights: Creation Centered Night Prayer* by Daniel J. McGill. Copyright © 1993 by Daniel J. McGill. Used by permission of Paulist Press.

Page 138: "Unbidden came God's love," from *Borrowed Light* by Thomas H. Troeger. Copyright © Oxford University Press. Used by permission.

Page 139: "God, help us to enter into the troubles," from *Plain Prayers in a Complicated World* by Avery Brooke. Copyright © 1993 Avery Brooke. Used by permission from Cowley Publications.

Page 139: "Give me, Lord, a stout heart," from *The SPCK Book of Christian Prayer*. Copyright © 1995 SPCK. Used by permission.

Page 139: James 5:16

Page 139: "You may call God love," from *Meditations with Meister Eckhart* by Matthew Fox. Copyright © 1983 Bear and Co. Used by permission.

Into Your Hands—Facing Death

Page 142: "Into your hands, O God, this solitude," from *Psalms of a Laywoman* by Edwina Gateley. Copyright © Edwina Gately. Used by permission.

Page 142: "I have always known," Author unknown.

Page 143: "Always, before this, I've just been sick," from *Plain Prayers in a Complicated World* by Avery Brooke. Copyright © 1993 Avery Brooke. Used by permission from Cowley Publications.

Page 143: "Let us live in such a way," from *The Prayer Tree* by Michael Leunig. Copyright © 1973 Michael Leunig. Used by permission of HarperCollins, Australia.

Pages 144–145: "The word of death curves around my heart," by Diane Berke. Copyright © 1996 Diane Berke. Used by permission of the author.

Page 146: "O Lord God, great distress has come upon me," from *Prayers from Prison* by Dietrich Bonhoeffer. Copyright © 1978 Fortress Press. Used by permission.

Page 146: "Father, my Father," Mark 14.

Page 147: "I worry and I wish," from *Right Side Up! Reflections for Those Living with Serious Illness* by Marlene Halpin. Copyright © 1995 Marlene Halpin. Used by permission of Islewest Publishing.

Page 147: "Go into the light and do not look back," used by permission of Sean Caulfield and America Press, New York, NY. Originally published in *America*, Feb. 29, 1992.

Page 148: "Lord, I am ill and I don't know what is wrong," from *It's Me O Lord* by Michael Hollings and Etta Gullick. Copyright © 1973 by Michael Hollings and Etta Gullick. Used by permission of Doubleday a division of Bantam Doubleday Dell Publishing Group and McCrimmon Publishing, Great Wakering, Essex.

Page 148: "Lord, If I have to die," from *Sometimes I Weep: Prayers and Meditations* by Ken Walsh. Copyright © 1973 Ken Walsh. Used by permission.

Page 149: "Pain isolates," from *Green Winter* by Elsie Maclay. Copyright © 1977 Elise Maclay. Administered and used by permission of Sanford J. Greenburger & Associates.

Page 149: "My boat is very small," from *Songs from Prison: Translations of Indian Lyrics Made in Jail* by M.K. Ghandi adapted by John S. Hoyland. Copyright © 1934 George Allen and Unwin.

Page 150: "O Lord, I've turned my eyes and my prayers to you," from *Your Words i n Prayer in Time of Illness* by Father Arnaldo Pangrazzi. Copyright © 1982 Alba House. Used by permission.

Page 150: "How to make these last days count," from *Plain Prayers in a Complicated World* by Avery Brooke. Copyright © 1993 Avery Brooke. Used by permission of Cowley Publications.